MOTOR DISORDERS

Robert Piazza
Assistant Professor of Special Education, Southern
Connecticut State College, New Haven, Connecticut.

Special Learning Corporation

42 Boston Post Rd. Guilford, Connecticut 06437

Special Learning Corporation

Publisher's Message:

The Special Education Series is the first comprehensive series designed for special education courses of study. It is also the first series to offer such a wide variety of high quality books. In addition, the series will be expanded and up-dated each year. No other publications in the area of special education can equal this. We stress high quality content, a superb advisory and consulting group, and special features that help in understanding the course of study. In addition we believe we must also publish in very small enrollment areas in order to establish the credibility and strength of our series. We realize the enrollments in courses of study such as Autism, Visually Handicapped Education, or Diagnosis and Placement are not large. Nevertheless, we believe there is a need for course books in these areas and books that are kept up-to-date on an annual basis! Special Learning Corporation's goal is to publish the highest quality materials for the college and university courses of study. With your comments and support we will continue to do this.

John P. Quirk

First Edition

1 2 3 4 5

ISBN No. 0-89568-088-2

CONTENTS

GLOSSARY OF TERMS

Auditory perception The ability to organize and interpret what is heard through the ear.

Brain damage A structural injury to the brain which may occur before, during, or after birth and which impedes the normal learnings process.

Central nervous system In humans, the brain and spinal cord to which sensory impulses are transmitted.

Conceptualization The ability to formulate concepts by inferring from what is observed.

Decoding The ability to understand what is expressed verbally or visually.

Discrimination The ability to perceive differences among stimuli presented visually (shapes) or auditorily (sounds).

Dyslexia-This term is usually associated with some brain dysfunction. It refers to the inability to learn to read or understand what is read.

Encode The expression of meaning in symbols or codes.

Etiology The source or origin of a condition.

Figure-ground perception The ability to attend to one part of a stimulus in relation to the rest of the field.

Hyperactivity Excessive and constant movement.

Hypoactivity An extreme lack of movement or listlessness.

Memory The ability to store and retrieve upon demand previously experienced sensation and perceptions.

Minimal brain dysfunction A mild neurological impairment that causes learning difficulties in the child with near-average intelligence.

Perception The process of organizing or interpreting stimuli received through the senses.

Perception of position The perception of the size and movement of an object in relation to the observer.

Perception of spatial relationships The perception of the positions of two or more objects in relation to each other.

Perceptual disorder A Disturbance in the awareness of objects, relations, or qualities, involving the interpretation of sensory stimuli.

Psycholinguistics The field of study that combines the disciplines of psychology and linguistics to examine the total language process.

Soft neurological signs The behavioral symptoms that suggest possible minimal brain inury in the absence of hard neurological signs.

Vestibular Pertaining to the sensory mechanism for the perception of the organism's relation to gravity.

Visual-motor The ability to coordinate visual stimuli with the movements of the body or its parts.

Visual perception The ability to identify, organize, and interpret what is received by the eye.

PREFACE

Motor disorders can be looked upon from three major viewpoints: *(1) developmental motor disabilities* such as spatial awareness difficulties, laterality, and directionality problems, and confusions of body image; *(2) hyperactive motor disorders* that have as their major characteristics restlessness, impulsivity, and uncoordinated movement; and *(3) physical disabilities* such as cerebral palsy and muscular dystrophy.

Readings in Motor Disorders will provide the reader with appropriate literature concerning the first two of these motor problems. They were chosen because learning disability specialists often must remediate children who demonstrate these difficulties. Individuals working in adaptive physical education programs and professionals interested in managing behavioral difficulties may also benefit from these readings.

While programs that concentrate solely on the development of motoric skills must be avoided in our schools, it must be realized that proficient movement skills are a necessary prerequisite to overall development.

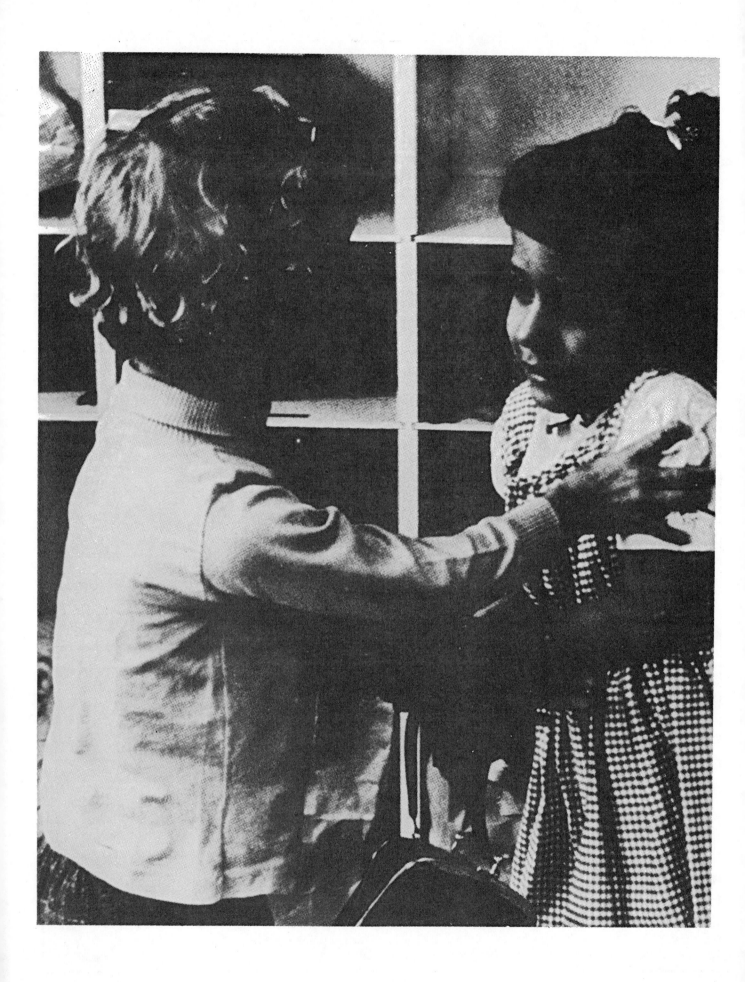

Developmental Motor Disorders

Since the work of Strauss in the 1930's and 1940's there has been increased attention paid to the child with developmental motor problems. His early work has led to the numerous ideas that have been offered by such individuals as Kephart, Barsch, Doman and Delacato, and Getman.

Most theorists in this area believe that the earliest learnings of a child are in the motor areas and these skills form the foundation for the attaining of later abilities. In fact, Kephart suggests that motor development evolves in a series of stages with each succeeding stage more complex than the preceding one.

Recently, training of motor skills by learning disability specialists has come under attack by researchers in the field. It had been thought that motor training would lead to the acquisition of academic tasks. This assumption has proven to be erroneous. It appears that many children who do not perform well motorically can function quite well in subjects such as reading, spelling and math.

The development of motor skills for their own sake is warranted, however. Being able to control ones body with efficiency is most advantageous in today's world. The following points illustrate the need for solid motor skills:

1. Physical health-the child who performs well motorically will engage in activities that may keep the child in good physical condition.
2. Socialization skills-individuals who display motor efficiency may become part of a peer group that can improve social adjustment. The child stands less of a chance of becoming isolated socially.
3. Self-concept--often a child's conception of himself is tied to the motor skills that have been developed. The youngster can also become more self-reliant and independent.

Because motor development is controllable in most cases, serious attention must be paid to it. The learning disability specialist in coordination with other individuals in the schools such as physical education teachers, should plan, implement, and evaluate motor development programs.

AROUSAL ATTENTION AND CONTROL

Bryant J. Cratty, Ed.D.

Professor of Physical Education
University of California, Los Angeles

Experimental psychologists, shortly after the turn of the century, discovered a principle which has been reconfirmed in innumerable studies during the subsequent years (23)(33). Essentially, the findings of these investigations pointed out that there is an optimum level of excitation or arousal which is productive of the best performance in a given task (28)(62). This level, of course, varies from task to task. Thus an individual's effectiveness in a given task is dependent upon the degree to which his level of arousal corresponds to the demands of the task. At times this level may be manipulated by the individual himself. In fact, it might be said that a truly intelligent and well-adjusted individual is one who may adjust his own level of arousal quickly and appropriately to the task demands made by confronting him at a given moment. This principle of optimum arousal may be graphed as follows:

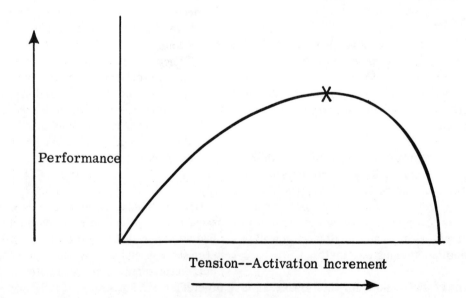

Maintaining an appropriate level of arousal enables an individual to devote his attention to the task rather than exhibiting distractable behavior, or being too withdrawn to react to the external stimuli. Thus optimum arousal usually elicits good attention to the task and attention to the learning task is probably more important to the learning of a task than the number of practice trials engaged in (66)(83). It is thus believed that what is critical to learning is self-control, the achievement of optimum arousal level, and the resultant attentive attitude taken toward the task, whether it be mental, clerical, or motor in nature.

It is not unusual to find, within groups of children classified as normal or as atypical, individuals who have difficulty controlling themselves (98). At times this lack of self-control may be due to emotional difficulties, and at other times due to some kind of subtle organic deficiency in the manner in which the nervous system functions. Among normal pre-school children it is not unusual to find that many lack impulse control, thus making learning difficult. Petri, in a series of exploratory studies, has suggested that there are two perceptual types (75). One type, the "augmenters" of stimuli, was described in the previous chapter, the other type is the "reducers" of stimuli. It is likely that the latter is the hyperactive, less sensitive child who finds sitting still in the traditional learning environment difficult, because of a lack of ability to adequately control his own level of arousal.

Among atypical groups of children, the incidence of individuals with problems controlling their hyperactivity and of focusing their attention on learning tasks is even greater. Zeaman and House have formulated a theoretical framework which places a large degree of emphasis upon this deficiency in retardates, in explaining their inability to learn (99).

It is obvious to any educator of the normal or atypical child that over-arousing children is relatively easy. In fact, most of the school's events activate children. The vigorous playground games usually induce levels of activation in children which are too high for effective concentration in classrooms. Classroom tasks which are stressful because of their complexity or difficulty similarly may over arouse children with defective nervous systems or disturbed personalities.

The over-aroused child does not often learn best under the classroom conditions usually found in elementary school. Better readers are usually children who are quiet and introspective (63). Children with higher I.Q.'s are the same children who seem able to move slowly when asked to do so (65). Retarded children who have difficulty attending to tasks for prolonged periods of time, even when novel conditions are introduced, have difficulty in learning (83). Calm and attentive babies have been found to be likely to evidence higher I.Q.'s in later life than the too active infant (3).

General activity level seems related to body build. The more muscular boy is likely to be more active (53). Moreover, general level of activity seems to some degree inherited. Scarr, for example, found relatively high correlations between measures of activity elicited from identical twins (84). These measures included the number of active games they chose, reaction times, and measures of anxiety and patience (84). There also is evidence that from birth infants are extremely variable in the quantity of activity they evidence (45). Irwin, for example, found that "busy" infants are 150 times more active than passive ones (45).

At the same time, within limits, it seems possible to apply various methods which will, to some degree, aid a child to adjust his level of activation. For example, hyperactivity and attention span in a classroom were found to be controllable in one investigation through the use of social reinforcement (2). In this investigation, a case study was carried out using a hyperactive four and one-half-year-old as a subject. At the beginning of the study his attention span was about one minute. After a period of training, during which immediate social approval was extended when the child paid attention to his lessons, his attention span lengthened to almost two minutes. When this kind of reinforcement was removed, his attention span regressed again to under one minute (fifty-three seconds), and when approval for attentive behavior was again instituted his attention span this second time increased to two and one-half minutes!

While life's stresses, as has been mentioned, are likely to raise arousal level, there are relatively few techniques available to the teacher which are likely to lower levels of activation to those appropriate to classroom tasks. Methodologies for accomplishing this (one popular in this country and the other in Europe) were both developed by physicians. The German psychiatrist, Shultz, in his 1959 text titled Autogenic Training (Self Training) and the American, Jacobsen, in his 1938 book titled Progressive Relaxation have advanced similar techniques (85)(47).

Generally these methods involve aiding the individual to become aware of extra muscular tensions within his body by asking him to alternately tighten and relax the total body and various muscle groups. Schultz's technique also emphasized breath control accompanied by the suggestion that various body parts are becoming warmer.

Jacobsen's methods have been subjected to varying degrees of clinical and experimental attention. In recent texts titled Anxiety and Tension Control and Tension in Medicine, Jacobson has cited evidence supplied by psychiatrists and others which suggest that his methods of tension control are affective of improvement in a variety of psychological and physical parameters. In an investigation by Johnson, using 48 psychiatric patients and relaxation training lasting ten minutes each day, it was found that a significant reduction in various indices of anxiety were achieved (various physiological measures of stress due to an immediate situation). Other measures of what were called "trait" anxiety, however, were not affected by Jacobson's relaxation training (51). (Anxiety as evaluated via questionnaire.)[1]

It seems reasonable to hypothesize, however, that if a consistent reduction is achieved in measures of situational anxiety, that general "trait" anxiety will similarly be likely to be affected over prolonged periods of time. It is hoped that additional longitudinal research on this question will be carried out.

It seems, however, that Jacobson's techniques provide a sound basis for the reduction of arousal level in a classroom or within a clinical setting. In addition to this, the research cited by Maccoby

-----
[1]Using Taylor's Manifest Anxiety Scale.

offers additional guidelines for the reduction of tension and the promotion of attention and impulse control. A further technique which we have found helpful in our program for neurologically-impaired children at the University of California, Los Angeles, involves attempts to motivate children to engage in motor tasks for prolonged periods of time—for periods of time longer than they have engaged in at any type of task before.

These three techniques will be briefly outlined and explained on the pages which follow.

Relaxation Training

The child should be placed in a position comfortable for him. He may be asked to lie on the floor, or to place his head on a desk. This positioning may be accompanied by soft music or music may be absent. When he is comfortable he should then be asked to alternately tighten his total body, first as hard as he can (he may be asked to "make the muscle hard" or other terms appropriate to the age and intellectual level of the child). This tightening should be held for from four to six seconds, and then be followed by directions to "relax completely" to make his muscles soft, or to "sink into the mat" or whatever verbal imagery is likely to communicate meaning to the child.

After the total body has been tightened to its fullest extent several times, alternated with periods of relaxation of slightly longer duration (five to ten seconds), the child should be asked to tighten his body "one-half that hard" and again each of these should be followed by periods of complete relaxation. If the children are sophisticated enough, the body should then be tightened one-half as hard as was done in the previous phase (one-fourth of maximum) followed by periods of relaxation.

After work with the total body has been carried out for four or more minutes, the child should be accustomed to tightening and relaxing various body parts. It is best to start near the head and progress downward, working with the face, eyes ("close your eyes as tightly as you can"), neck muscles, shoulder muscles, and so on. Again the child should be asked to exert full effort, one-half effort, and one-fourth effort if he is able to do so.

The final portions of the time should again be taken up with directions to exert all out, one-half, and one-fourth effort in tightening the muscles of the total body. The rest periods between these efforts should be occupied with directions to breathe deeply and slowly.

After children have engaged in this type of training for prolonged periods of time, it is possible for some of them to apply these methods to themselves. However, in most cases the teacher or clinician must continue to provide the stimulus.

Impulse Control

Following a "session" of relaxation training it is often useful to determine how effectively the child is able to control the tempo and rate of his own movements. He should be directed to move as slowly as he can in a number of activities including movement of the total body, i.e. "How slowly can you get up?", "How slowly can you get down?", and so on; movement of the limbs, i.e. "How slowly can you raise your hands over your head?"; and in writing movements, i.e. "How slowly can you draw a line from here to there?"

Often competition may be used to elicit this type of controlled activity. Two or more children, for example, may be started from a back-lying position on the mat. When told to "go" they must "race" to see who can get up slowest. The winner (the child up first) thus becomes the loser! Using graphic movements, the children may be placed at opposite ends of a narrow "road" drawn on a board, and each asked to draw a line toward each other, each attempting to move slower than his partner. Two or more children may be placed on lines, and asked to see how slowly they can walk them. The ones finishing first are thus the losers.

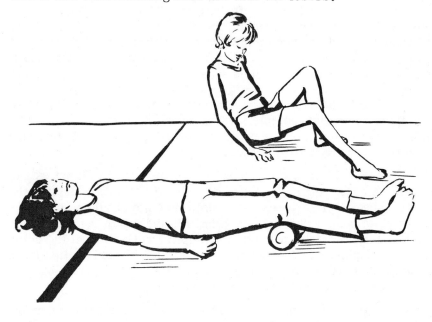

Several principles must be kept in mind when engaging in this type of training. The tasks must be reasonably difficult, or the child may be noted to be controlling his motor actions, (i.e. walking the line), while his attention (visual regard) is maintained elsewhere. Thus a child may be asked to walk a line and over a rope which crosses the line periodically, or to draw between lines placed closely together on the blackboard, so that the task requires his close visual attention.

Furthermore, when the child first moves he must continue moving, rather than stopping and starting in order to best his competition. (It may be necessary when working with extremely hyperactive children to reinforce them with external reinforcers for periods of complete immobility, prior to engaging in this type of impulse-control activity.)

It will also be found that many of these tasks, such as getting up slowly, require a great deal of physical effort. It may be true, therefore, that they may heighten rather than lower general arousal level, despite the amount of self-control they require.

It may become apparent, particularly when working with extremely suggestible children, that this type of training is not eliciting a flexible type of response pattern. They may begin to move too slowly in many situations, instead of adjusting their movement speed to levels appropriate to the task confronting them.

It is therefore necessary, after it is seen that the child can control his movement speed in a number of tasks, to ask him to move as rapidly as he can, and then to determine if he can again place himself under good control. Instructions such as "How fast can you get up?" may thus be alternated with such directions as "Get up as slowly as you can" during the latter stages of this type of training program.

Prolonging Tasks

Gross and fine motor tasks are activities whose duration and speed are easily discernible. An observing teacher may easily see when a child starts a task of this nature and when he terminates his efforts. It has been found within our program for atypical children at the University of California, Los Angeles, that simply asking children or motivating them with social and monetary reinforcers to engage in tasks for prolonged periods of time has reduced their hyperactivity.

A task sometimes used is line walking. The child is required to walk lines of increasing length on successive days. Another task involves keeping a ball on the back of a square piece of wood (two feet by two feet) for increasing periods of time. Line drawing tasks have also been used and a stop watch informs the child as well as his instructor how long he has engaged in this graphic behavior on successive trials and on succeeding days.

It is important to inform a child of his improvement in this kind of exercise if he is capable of understanding. At the same time a graphic record may be presented to the child depicting his progress.

Relaxation training, impulse control activities, as well as the latter tasks which involve prolonging the duration of time in which tasks are engaged in should be practiced initially in conditions which are relatively bland. After some success is realized, conditions which are likely to raise the child's level of arousal may be introduced and training reinstituted. For example, after a child has begun to take several seconds to draw a line, another child might be brought in to observe him. Various kinds of auditory stressors may similarly be introduced into the training situations in order to aid the child to control his activities under more distractive conditions. For example, he may be asked to move slowly while a conversation is being carried out near him.

Initially, quieting music may be beneficial for relaxation training and when impulse control activities are practiced. However, when the child begins to evidence improvement in these activities more stimulating music may be played.

Summary

Control of level of arousal and activation seems critical to the learning process. Hyperactive children are invariably beset with learning difficulties, while an index of intelligence and emotional stability is good self control. Three types of activities were outlined which were designed to aid children to place themselves under better control and to aid them to attend better to classroom tasks and to tasks within the succeeding chapters in this text. These activities included relaxation techniques involving the control of muscular tensions within the body, impulse control activities which require the child to move slowly in various tasks and prolonging tasks for increased periods of time. While it is true that these more obvious types of motor behavior are not always perfectly correlated with emotional arousal, it is usual to find that they are helpful in reducing hyperactivity in atypical children and in normal children who have difficulty attending to educational tasks.

Yoga In Psychomotor Training

Laura J. Hopkins
J. Thomas Hopkins

Laura J. Hopkins, MEd, is a resource teacher in the Hamilton County Public Schools, Chattanooga, Tennessee 37401. J. Thomas Hopkins, EdD, is assistant professor in the School of Education, University of Tennessee at Chattanooga, Chattanooga, Tennessee 37401.

THE PSYCHOMOTOR DOMAIN is an area which has received a great amount of attention in special education in recent years with the increase in concern for developing programs for children with learning disabilities. Many educators give psychomotor programing a central place in their curricula. Others, while not centering on psychomotor training, include it as part of their programs. The reasons for the inclusion of psychomotor training in special education programs vary; but it is clear that many of the children served in special education programs are weak--not only in academic skills, but in motor skills as well. A direct link between psychomotor functioning and proficiency in academic skills has yet to be clearly demonstrated; but even in the absence of such a demonstrated link, it is clear that many children are able to derive benefit from psychomotor activities. Bryant Cratty has stressed the need for further exploration in to the relationship between bodily movement and the learning process.[1]

We would like to suggest that a modified program of yoga can be of great benefit to children, especially ones with psychomotor deficits, when used as an adjunct to, or even as the central core of, a psychomotor program. An experimental study is presently underway to explore these possibilities. A simplified yoga program can offer many of the advantages to be found in psychomotor programs already in existence. Yoga postures can promote body awareness, balance, laterality, and crossing the midline—points which have been stressed by such educators as Newell C. Kephart and Cratty.[2] Yoga can also offer a distinct advantage in that it can provide a definite calming effect which can help the child into a frame of mind which is conducive to learning.

Calming Effects

The development of muscle tone and coordination are planned into the total program of every child in school. Some children served by special programs can easily fit into a regular physical education program, often with only slight modification. There are children, however, who are reluctant to participate in a regular program because they are self-conscious about their lack of coordination and general difficulty performing physical tasks. There are also some children who seem to "wind up" when participating in physical activity. Teachers speak of such a child as "getting silly" and "unable to control himself." These children are seen as ones who cannot settle down to classroom activities for a long period after physical activity. It is for these children that we plan developmental psychomotor programs. It is with this group that yoga can have a distinct advantage over other forms of physical activity. Also, a yoga program can be developed to meet the individual needs of the students. Very tense children can gain a great deal from the spine-stretching exercises which are a central part of yoga. The postures themselves are relaxing to the tense body, and students often comment on the feeling of well-being.

Slow Controlled Movement

Yoga is, by nature, not a strenuous activity program. Muscle tone and development are part of yoga; but these goals are reached by means of slow, deliberate movement. The emphasis in yoga is on slow, carefully controlled movement rather than just getting body parts from one position to another or thrusting of the body about with various amounts of force, as is the case with some activity programs. It is a common misconception that the emphasis in physical yoga is the achievement of certain physical postures. In actuality, the *process of movement* involved in approximating the postures is a more important feature. Through modified yoga exercises children can become more aware of their bodies in space as well as more aware of their bodily tensions which the yoga exercises help to release.

Breathing

Controlled breathing is an important part of all exercises in yoga. Children are taught to breathe from the diaphragm which promotes a more efficient exchange of oxygen and carbon dioxide. This also has the effect of making children more conscious of their own bodies. Children respond well to these kinds of activities. The writers have noted the remarkable calming effect that these exercises can have on children.

Practical Advantages

In addition to the advantages to the children, there are a number of practical considerations which make a modified yoga program attractive. Teachers who would like to work with such a program do not need to become yogis in order to carry it out. When the subject of yoga is brought up, the image which comes to the minds of some persons is of a skinny little Indian man who ties himself in knots. While it is preferred that the teacher be able to demonstrate the exercises for the children, even a beginner will find that the modified program we use can be followed with ease by most teachers. It should be kept in mind that the children will be beginners in the program also. The program does not involve strenuous activity. There is no goal which must be reached. Muscles are simply extended to their limit so that there is a slight stretching; the position is then held for a few seconds.

In our experimental program, the program has even proved to be of benefit to the teacher. Leading the children through the exercise program has, on a number of occasions, relieved the tensions of the teacher who had had a very trying morning. On these occasions the teacher reported that she felt much calmer and more in control after the yoga session than she had before the psychomotor period.

Another practical advantage is that there is no special equipment involved, so that the program has very little cost involved with it. It is a good idea to have a mat or a carpeted floor, but these are often available in schools already.

Response from the elementary school children has been encouraging. As the exercises are described, images of familiar animals and objects are used; and the child is encouraged to use his imagination as he moves into the posture. As children pretend to be a frightened cat, it is easy for them to keep their backs arched for several seconds in order to gain maximum release of tension. Junior high and high school children can perform the exercises on a more mature level. As tension is relieved by the various postures and muscle tone improves, the program becomes rewarding in and of itself.

Modification for Children

Yoga exercises can be developed into an interesting activity for children of all ages. Rachel Carr has presented yoga exercises "thru mimicry, such as pretending to be a jumping frog, a flying bird, a shooting arrow, or a hopping crow."[3] This approach is very fruitful and can be expanded upon by a creative teacher and her students. We, too, have adapted selected yoga exercises for a class of noncategorized, special-needs, primary-aged children. Selection and modification of exercises is important. Yoga exercises, as they are presented in the many yoga manuals now available, are often not well suited for the use of young children. A number of the standard yoga exercises are too difficult and, as a result, have a tendency to increase tension in the children rather than to reduce it.

The program we developed involves the use of imagery which most young children relate to easily. For example, in one of the exercises the children are told to imagine that they are in a jar of peanut butter—very thick peanut butter. Their movements have to be very slow because they have to push the peanut butter out of their way. This is a good beginning exercise. It is basically a stretching exercise to limber up the spine and to make the point that movements in yoga are to be slow and deliberate, never rushed, always as if walking in a jar of peanut butter. Almost all of the children are successful with this exercise.

In another exercise, the children are told that they are going to become airplanes. They make their bodies into airplanes by spreading their arms. Then they are told to imagine that they are coming upon some mountains and must maneuver around them. They must bank the plane slowly to the left and then to the right. As they proceed, the mountains become higher, and they must bank more steeply. Finally they must bank so steeply that one wing is straight up in the air and the other pointing toward the ground. Of course these movements must be done slowly, so that the passengers and cargo are not shaken up. This exercise is also a relatively easy exercise for most children.

Results

We have seen some encouraging results from the experimental study. Not only have teachers involved in the program noted improvement in the tension states of the children involved, but other teachers in the school can note the difference between the children who have been doing yoga and those who have been involved in other activities. They note that the yoga group seems much more relaxed. These remarks have been made by teachers who did not know which children were engaged in what activity. These preliminary observations suggest that there are some definite advantages to including some modified yoga exercises in a psychomotor program.

NOTES

1. B. Cratty, *Perceptual-Motor Behavior and Education Processes* (Springfield, Illinois: Charles C Thomas, 1969).
2. N. C. Kephart, *The Slow Learner in the Classroom* (2nd ed.) (Columbus, Ohio: Charles E. Merrill, 1971); Cratty, *op. cit.*
3. R. Carr, *Be a Frog, a Bird, or a Tree* (Garden City, New York: Doubleday & Company, 1973).

Learning Through Movement

Patrick A. O'Donnell

San Anselmo Schools

Movement Exploration

When left free to do so, children have always engaged in some form of movement exploration. When provided with an adequate physical *environment,* including the amount, kind, and arrangement of space, they tend to engage in the types of physical activity which are optimum for their individual levels of physical development. Recently, educators have begun to examine more closely the educative possibilities inherent in this childhood "phenomena" of *movement exploration.*

Systematic attention to movement exploration appears to have begun in England approximately twenty-five years ago. During the intervening years, the concept has been developed in breadth and depth and extensive programs have been developed by English physical educators. Most of these programs place much stress on the need for children to have opportunities to study basic body movement at an early age. Appropriate experience with movement is provided through selective exposure to developmental and exploratory movement activities.

Through movement experiences, the child becomes more cognizant of the potential range of movement possible with his body. He learns which movements are possible at his individual level of development and which require postural-locomotor responses which are too complex or are impossible. Through exploratory activities, he develops insights about body mechanics which enable or constrict movement. As he develops new means for solving movement problems, he develops greater ease and confidence in his motor abilities. The generalization drawn from the movement experience will provide much of the *effective power* of the training since these can be applied to other learning. Thus, instead of isolated instruction on each new skill, the movement components of the skill can be identified and the generalization from previous experience can be applied.

With practice, the child gains insight into the influence of various extrinsic and intrinsic factors on movement. The child who inadvertently knocks articles off tables or shelves may not be able to move efficiently or appropriately through the kind or quality of space available.

Finally, through movement exploration, the child can experience the joy of movement. Since success can be assured if the instruction is developmental and individualized, the child's self-concept may be enhanced. If success has the expected effects on self-confidence and self-concept, the child is likely to be more willing to attempt new and more complex skills. Outcomes such as the following have been reported frequently after movement exploration experiences:

> children feel successful,
>
> children gain respect for the abilities of self and others,
>
> children express emotions freely through movement,
>
> children develop a sense of daring, adventure, and innovation,
>
> children who are shy or withdrawn are able to express themselves through movement.

In brief, movement exploration can be defined as planned problem-solving experiences. Through problems which progress in complexity and difficulty, the child learns to understand and control the many possibilities for movement provided by his body. Through better understanding and control of his body, the child is able to achieve higher levels of performance on a variety of motor skills. Movement exploration or movement education is not meant to be the total physical education program in the elementary school. It is one approach to instruction in basic skills which involve some dimensions of bodily movement. When planned in an imaginative fashion, movement problems not only assist in the development of useful skills but also provide vigorous, satisfying activity. Thus, activities which stress invention, imagination, and problem solving must be planned. While physical traits such as strength, endurance, and speed may improve as a concomitant of movement activity, they should not be the focus or primary emphasis of the program.

The individual development of each student is of paramount importance in movement exploration. Competition and quantitative criteria are usually *not* an integral part of the activity. Rather, activities must be evaluated in terms of the degree to which they contribute to the child's understanding of the mechanics of his body and the degree to which they enable him to move more effectively and efficiently through space.

There is no single correct response or solution to a problem. Rather solutions are evaluated on an individual basis in terms of whether they are more adaptive, effective, or insightful than previous solutions reached by the same individual. Identical movements are not possible for all individuals because of basic differences in physiological development, experience, and similar factors. Identical or similar solutions may not be equally adaptive or insightful. A large measure of success and positive reinforcement is possible for every child because of the wide latitude in alternative solutions.

In movement exploration, precise introduction of new skills is not as vital or critical as is the analysis of errors. A careful analysis of errors during the early stages of practice will enable the teacher to provide a maximum of assistance to pupils as they attempt to improve their movement potentials. The child needs to understand the functioning of his joints, muscles, leverage, and similar elements of body mechanics. Through a variety of methods of feedback, the teacher enables the child to develop increased understanding and control of these principles. As with most learning, the principles should, in turn, be generalizable to the learning of new and more specific skills. It is in the presumed *transfer* to the learning of other skills with subsequent accelerated mastery of these skills that the hypothetical efficacy of movement experience lies.

In order to provide effective instruction, the teacher must be aware of some fundamentals of movement. Basic movement patterns can be analyzed from at least four perspectives (Schurr, 1967). *Qualities of Movement* represent one dimension of concern. Is the movement rapid, slow, intermittent, accelerating, or decelerating. Is the body in an open or closed position? How much force is appropriate for proper execution of the movement? Is the movement continuous and open-ended or are there well defined points of closure? What is the optimum configuration of the body? Application of data on factors such as body configuration to motor skills such as skiing should be apparent. Postural factors such as stability are dependent on the maintenance of appropriate body position. The child can explore the effectiveness of various postural adjustments through guided movement experience.

A second perspective for the study of movement is provided through an analysis of *space*. What direction is the body moving? Are there differences in the effectiveness of the body as it moves in different directions? How does the stability or balance of the body change during upward, downward, or sideward movement? As the child explores various movement, he will be discovering relationships between the center of gravity and the base of support of his body. Thus, when the body is in a low position, the center of gravity will be close to the base of support and balance should be enhanced. The child will have opportunities to discover differences in balance between forward and backward movement. Principles of postural adjustment, body image, coordination, laterality, and so forth can be identified and improved through guided movement experience.

Body actions provide a third set of variables for the analysis of movement. Which locomotor or non-locomotor actions or combinations are required for the successful execution of the movement? Does the body need to be in a position to initiate, receive, or transfer weight? A task analysis similar to that which was illustrated earlier for running should be helpful in pointing out specific errors to the child.

Less important but noticeable variation can be provided through an analysis of *relationships*. Some movements such as lifting, swinging, and leaping can be facilitated or enriched through planned participation with partners or in small or large groups. The pattern of movement required for lifting in conjunction with another person differs from the patterns required when the child lifts alone. Sliding in cadence with another adds elements of control and planning which are less important when the child slides alone. Group activities such as "leap frog" provide many opportunities for naturalistic practice.

Planning Movement Experience

Instruction in movement exploration will differ for younger and older pupils. Older children may explore and study specific factors in movement as an end or objective. Learning will progress as the older child experiments with movements and explores the potentialities and limitations of each. Frequently, the opportunity to modify older movement patterns or to learn new ones is sufficient incentive to insure the continued interest and participation of older children. On the other hand, movement exploration is more effective with younger pupils when the activities involve some dramatic content or purposes. New movements are attempted as the young child attempts to express new purposes.

Not	*Rather*
Stand on your toes.	See if you can touch the ceiling.
Jump as far as you can.	Jump over the wide river in front of you.
Swing your arm in a circle.	See if you can make a propellor out of your arm.

For more effective movement training, focus on the elements of movement:

Purpose:	*Relationships:*
Spatial Relationships:	— Why do we move?
Quality of Movement:	— Where do we move?
Body Mechanics:	— How do we move?
	— What is moving?
	— With whom do we move?

In addition to the above suggestion, there are some further cautions which should be helpful.

- *Do not demonstrate*
  Movement exploration is a problem solving experience. A demonstration represents a solution which is likely to be limited.

- *Repeated presentation of the same problem may be helpful.*
  Children should be encouraged to experiment with *alternative* solutions to the same problem. The effectiveness of the training may be increased if children are encouraged to compare solutions achieved.

- *Children should wear clothes which allow free movement. Children should be barefoot.*
  Solutions should not be rejected because clothes are inappropriate. Muscles, joints, and other factors of body mechanics, not clothes, should provide the constraints on movement.

- *Encourage original responses.*
  Directions should be broad and open-ended. Use verbal reforcement to encourage original responses.

- *Use rhythm instruments sparingly at first*
  The child should learn to develop cadence and timing without the assistance of a beat. The introduction of rhythm will also provide a constraint on the variety of responses attempted.

Perceptual-Motor Learning

Body Image

Rope Activities

Place four pieces of ½" rope about 8' long between desks. Each segment is stretched between two desks with segments parallel to each other and about 18" apart. Start ropes close to the floor and gradually move upward.

Sample Directions:

1. Walk forward over the ropes
2. Crawl under the ropes
3. Walk sideways over the ropes
4. Walk backwards over the ropes
5. Hop over the ropes (one foot)
6. Crawl over the ropes forward, backward, sidewards.

Place ropes at different heights.

1. Walk over the first rope, under the second, etc.
2. Walk over the first rope, crawl under the second, etc.

Continue with similar variations.

Drawing Activities
Draw a group picture of a human figure. The first child can start and each successive child can add a part or member.

Robot Man
Move around the room in a mechanical fashion. "Freeze" on signal and then begin again on command.

Slow-Motion Movies
Perform various movements around the room as if caught in slow motion.

Where Toucher
One child stands at the front of the room, with eyes shut and back to room. A child is selected to come to the front and touch the child standing. Child must identify the part of the body touched (e. g., right side, back of head).

Free Movement
Child lies on the floor with his eyes closed. In response to verbal commands, child modifies body configuration without opening eyes. "See if you can look like a starfish."

Hand Activities
Stand facing another child with both hands joined. Children push and pull in alternating fashion.

Children can stand facing each other with both hands joined and then whirl rapidly.

Boys will enjoy Indian Wrestling. This activity involves intensive sensory stimulation.

Floor Activities
Children can roll across the floor or under a bar.
Children can crawl through tunnels, large pipes or under chairs.

Laterality

Simon Says
The familiar game of "Simon Says" provides many opportunities for practice and reinforcement on right and left.

Matching Hands
Outline a large number of hands on the chalkboard in differing positions. The child must attempt to place his hand over an outlined hand in the correct orientation.

Chalkboard Training
Child stands facing the chalkboard. Teacher (or another child) draws a dot. Child places his chalk on the dot. Teacher draws a second dot and child draws a line to second dot without raising the chalk from the board. Teacher continues with a third dot. When the child is able, dots should cross the midline of the body.

1. DEVELOPMENT

Tension-Relaxation

Mickey Mouse Balloon

From a position on the floor, have the child blow himself up (one part at a time) like a balloon. Then, have the child reverse the order allowing the air to escape until he resembles a limp balloon on the floor.

Stretch

Have the child stretch as high as he can and hold the position as long as he can—then release the body.

Moving on Signal

Have the children continue to move as long as there is a sound (drum, record, or piano). When the sound stops, the child should collapse quickly to the floor. Allow the child to practice this with differing tempos.

Stop on Signal

Have the child swing arms in an arc until drum beat or other sound stops. The object of this activity is to stop as quickly as possible. Similar experiences can be provided with running and walking.

Extremes

Child should experience the extremes in sensation. Stretch to the ceiling and then fall quickly and limply to the floor. Close the eyes and then attempt the same activity.

Butter

Ask the child to pretend that he is a stick of cold butter melting on a hot day.

Stretch

Have the child stretch all of the muscles he can until they ache. Then have the child release the muscles little by little.

Rag Doll

Have the child pretend he is a rag doll hanging on a clothesline.

Tense-Release

Have the child tense all of the body, one part at a time. Have him release the tension one part at a time and then remain still.

Balance

Color Identification

Pin a 4" square of colored construction paper on the back of one child. The second child must try to look behind the other and identify the color while hopping.

Stilts

Stilts provide excellent practice in balance. Coffee cans with ropes tied on either side make excellent stilts for use in school.

Puppet

Have the child stretch as high as he can, drop his arms and shoulders and attempt to move as if a string were attached to the top of his head.

Leaning

Leaning in a direction is a prelude to moving in that direction. The child can practice leaning:

lean forward while walking

take the longest step possible
lean backward and sideward
leand forward until balance is threatened

Ball Bounce

Make a bridge using two legs and one hand. Bounce a ball first with one hand and then the other.

Tight-Rope Walking

Walk slowly along a ten-foot chalk line with the arms extended sideward to assist in maintaining balance.

Balance Stand

Stand on either foot with body bent forward to right angle. Head should be up and arms extended for balance.

Coordination

Jumping Jack

From a squatting position, jump straight up until all of the body weight is on the heels.

Turk Stand

Stand straight with arms folded and legs crossed. Without bending the trunk of the body, slowly lower the body to a sitting position. Again, without bending, raise to a standing position.

Rabbit

From a bending position, place hands flat on the floor in front. With a small hop, bring the legs up to the hands. Again place the hands in front and bring the legs forward with a hop. Continue this sequence to maintain forward progression.

Duck Walk

From a squatting position with knees wide and hands placed under arm pits, child swings the feet wide to the side with each step and flaps wings.

Walking in Rhythm, Moving in Style

Teaching Fundamental Movement Patterns to Children with Learning Problems

RONALD W. SCHWORM

Ronald W. Schworm is on the educational psychology faculty at the State University of New York at Albany.

■ Because physical adeptness is deemed important by society many demands are made on children to perform various kinds of skills. The environments of some children, however, do not expose them to or require them to perform certain skills, while other children are exposed and encouraged to perform but do so with difficulty. Both kinds of children encounter problems in school environments and frequently need deliberate instruction if they are to participate in everyday activities with other children.

A project conducted at the Motor Learning and Development Laboratory at the University of Illinois tested strategies for teaching perceptual-motor tasks to school aged children who have difficulty performing particular movement patterns of skilled behavior. Instruction emphasized fundamental movement patterns that would not normally be demanded by the environment for survival: catching, throwing, jumping, and hopping. The following instructional procedures directly involve the student with skill related activities that are task oriented and goal directed.

MOVEMENT: TEACHING THE PROCESS AS PRODUCT

When defined for instructional purposes, *movement* means the entire task from beginning to end. A task would be an activity that uses a particular movement pattern and has a defined outcome; for example, throwing a ball underhand to a box, hopping from one square to another, bounce passing a ball to a target on a wall. By definition, each movement has two components: process and product. The process is the movement pattern, and the product is the outcome or end result of that movement pattern. Unless the process or movement pattern is efficient it is unlikely that any child will complete a movement task continuously and consistently. When movement is inefficient it is characterized by irrelevant, unorganized actions resulting in poor patterns. Children who are inefficient repeatedly display uncertainty, hesitancy, poor posture, and a lack of coordination and control when deliberately moving. Children who are ineffective performers are frequently inefficient and their task completion is repeatedly inaccurate and inconsistent; the target is not hit and the ball is not caught.

"MOVING VIOLATIONS"

When teaching movement patterns in a task oriented approach certain considerations need to be understood.

Most children who commit "moving violations" do so because of faulty movement habits. Many children do not adequately attend to the relevant actions needed to perform and complete a task. They are not aware of relevant stimuli to which to attend and respond when they are asked to correct or adjust a movement pattern. They imitate poorly and do not acquire correct behaviors by trial and error learning. Movement problems are often the result of lack of exposure to and deliberate experience with systematic and relevant instruction.

A child who displays immature neurological development or lacks neurological integrity can still become efficient. A child who does display some kind of impairment can still become competent when adjustments and directions emphasize the efficient features of a movement task and are adapted for individual differences.

MOVING WELL

Body position, posture, and cues that provide the most information for the child are more important than the activities themselves. Changing the position and posture of a child, for example, will usually improve balance and coordination quicker than continuous exercise on various pieces of equipment that stress "did you do it" rather than "how did you do it."

During instruction, the emphasis is on purposeful efficient movement patterns that are task related and goal directed. Orienting the movement to a target or goal makes deliberate movement more meaningful, increases attention and motivation, and, it is hoped, stimulates some imagination. The child who understands the actions of a movement pattern and who knows what is needed to complete a task learns to move more easily and more quickly.

READY TO MOVE

The child is asked to demonstrate functional movement patterns of skills as a part of whole tasks. The movement patterns of catching, overhand and underhand throwing, ball bouncing, ball passing, hopping, and jumping are observed, measured, and recorded while the child performs specified tasks. As the child throws a ball underhand to a box, for example, eye-hand coordination, position of limbs and head, anticipation of the movement, and the posture taken before, during, and after a movement are recorded (see Figure 1). Each task is completed more than once. During evaluation, continuous adjustments are made until the movement pattern approaches efficiency. Evaluation is continuous: observe, measure, record, *adjust*, observe, measure, record, *adjust*.

FIGURE 1   RECORD OF ASSESSMENT

Movement pattern: Underhand throw

Target: _____ Object: _____

Distance: _____

	1	2	3	4	5	6	7	8	9	10
Arm Swing										
Release										
Head position										
Eye-hand										
Timing										
Step										
Opposition										
Balance										
Position										

Trials

+ = Good
- = Poor or absent
-, + = Completed after adjustment

Movement:
Abortive ____
Jerky ____
Smooth ____
Preresponse:
Uncertain ____
Hesitant ____
Adequate ____

Comments:

WHAT TO TEACH: AN EXAMPLE

The objective of instruction is to have the student learn mature movement patterns. The mature movement pattern consists of actions that provide the necessary force, use the most relevant

"Walking in Rhythm, Moving in Style". Ronald W. Schworm, *Teaching Exceptional Children* Vol. 9, No. 2, Winter 1977 ©

muscle groups, and expend the least amount of energy. These actions are called invariant and can be learned. It is the invariant movement patterns that must become efficient if effectiveness of movement is to improve.

The following, for example, are the invariant actions of the underhand throw: With the ball in the preferred hand, the arm is brought down and back, extending out and along the body. The hand should just miss the leg. As the arm is brought forward the opposite foot and leg step forward, with the knee slightly bent. Release of the ball is made just before the arm is fully extended. Body weight is transferred to the stepping leg and foot. The head remains stable and is positioned so the eyes keep contact with the target. The feet should not lift.

TEACHING STRATEGY

Instruction is divided into two stages: (a) before the movement is activated and (b) during the movement.

Stage 1 involves selectively attending to the actions of a movement pattern. The teacher must become aware of the invariant actions needed to complete the movement pattern. Instruction directs the student's attention to the invariant actions. It is intended that the student acquire a visual image of the skill before it is performed, and initially it is critical to focus on the goal of the movement before concentrating on the specific movement pattern.

The teacher imitates the movement pattern and describes the actions. The child rehearses the whole of the movement pattern at a pace that does not interfere with timing. The teacher directs the student's attention by asking: Where will your arm go, how will it go, where will your leg go, what should your head do, and so forth. The student responds by describing the actions and demonstrating the positions of the body needed to perform the movement pattern efficiently.

Stage 2 involves selectively attending to the direction of movement pattern actions. Cues and commands are provided concurrently to direct attention to the movement pattern actions as they are being performed and immediately after the movement is completed. Some children may need strong, salient cues. For example, cues are presented to assist the child to make a "decision" on where and when to apply force, when to release, in which direction the arms and legs go, what arms and legs move together, and what position the body assumes. The cues provide external feedback to force the child to perform and monitor the movement pattern.

Features of a Teaching Strategy

Each execution of a movement pattern follows an established procedure, with emphasis placed on the following elements:
1. The set for the movement.
2. The command to move.
3. The invariant actions of the movement pattern.
4. The timing of the actions.
5. The target and goal.
6. The cues that may be needed.

An example of movement execution is shown in Figure 2.

Initially, movement patterns are done slowly so the student can use visual feedback to make adjustments. As movement patterns become programed and automatic, the amount of speed, force, and distance can be changed. Movement patterns are completed at a pace that does not result in loss of timing. A nice even pace must be established.

External cues are provided to assist the student with position, balance, force, timing, and pacing. Cues should be diminished and faded out gradually and used only until movement becomes self regulatory. Cues can be used to direct the movement pattern and to set pace. For example, having the child throw the ball over a horizontal pole to a target placed directly below will force the student to loft the ball slowly using a more mature movement pattern. Cues help decrease random actions that are not part of the invariant actions of a movement pattern. A strong cue helps a child know immediately if efficiency was achieved.

PRACTICE, SCORING, CHARTING

No more than 10 minutes should be spent on any one task. Practice and repetition with deliberate instruction is the key to improvement. Practice of the movement pattern precedes scoring for the chart. When the student feels ready the teacher should score. During practice time the teacher should correct and assist the student with the pattern. The total movement must be done each time the task is attempted.

NO SUPERSTARS

Teaching children movement skills should be fun for the child and the instructor. Learning should take place in a relaxed setting when the child is not tired. Classroom teachers, parents, and other students can provide instruction. The intent of instruction is to assist the child in learning to move efficiently and effectively when participating in skill related events. The goal is not to create a competitive athlete. Rather, the goal of instruction is to provide systematic and relevant procedures that will organize and coordinate a child's actions so that he or she may perform a functional perceptual-motor skill.

FIGURE 2

Example: Bouncing a Ball with the Preferred Hand while Stationary

EXECUTION OF A MOVEMENT

Set: Stand in the set position for throwing.

Command: "Ready . . . go."

Movement pattern: The ball is pushed using the fingers, and the whole arm is extended downward directing the ball to the target. The arm supplies the force. After the arm extends and the ball is pushed the arm recovers by bending at the elbow and is placed in a position so that the hand greets the ball and pushes it down again. The body should bend slightly at the waist so that eye contact can be made with the target and the ball. The feet may pivot but do not move from the set position.

Timing and pacing: The recovery of the arm must be timed to the amount of force applied. If the pace is fast and force is hard the arm and hand must reset quickly.

Ball and target: Use an air inflated 8 inch or larger utility ball, slightly deflated. A soft basketball is also useful. Make a large square or circle target from colored paper and position it in front of the child at the base of the feet.

Cues:
1. The ball is not slapped. To prevent slapping tape a piece of breakable candy to the palm of the pushing hand. If the ball is slapped the candy is broken. If done efficiently the student may eat the candy.
2. The arm must be extended downward. To provide the student with visual feedback fasten a piece of colored yarn at the wrist and shoulder when the arm is extended. After each push the yarn should be straight.
3. Count and clap to establish a rhythm and to keep time, if needed. Bounce another ball to set the pace.
4. Place tape strips across the tops of the shoes and fasten the ends to the floor. If the foot is moved the tape will break or pull up.

The Clumsy Child Syndrome: Some Answers To Questions Parents Ask

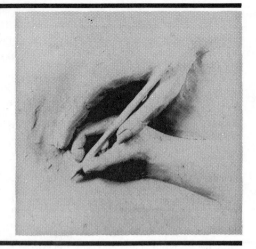

Bryant J. Cratty, Ed. D.

University of California At Los Angles 1973

The Author: Dr. Bryant J. Cratty is a Professor of Kinesiology at UCLA and Director of the Perceptual-Motor Learning Laboratory there. He is the author of over 30 books and monographs and of the section on "Sensory-Motor Learning" in the Encyclopedia Britannica. He is a consultant to the Bureau of Education for the Handicapped of the U.S. Department of Education, and also to over 20 school districts throughout the country. His writing deals with motor learning, the psychology of physical activity, and the use of movement experiences in the education of atypical children. His research has been sponsored by the National Science Foundation, the Bureau of Handicapped Children, U.S. Office of Education, a private Donor's Grant, University Research Grants, and by the Institute of Neurological Diseases and Blindness within the National Institutes of Health.

INTRODUCTION

During the past twelve years, we have conducted here at UCLA a program for the remediation of children with minor to moderate motor problems. The children are evaluated using a number of tests to assess the control of big muscles, writing behavior, as well as their self-concept and game choices. While the children are being individually tested, the parents and I observe, using a one-way mirror arrangement, during this period of time. Afterward, I explain the purposes of the testing and interpret test results to them.

As these observations are being carried out, there are a number of questions which are frequently directed toward me. Indeed, one can identify from 10-12 questions which occur with such regularity that I was prompted to write the short monograph which follows. Such questions range from relatively simple pragmatic ones, revolving around programs of activity and remediation, to other more complex ones delving into causes of motor disturbances which, in order to properly answer, require the expertise of a committee of neurologists,

pediatricians, psychiatrists, and child psychologists. Indeed, a
better sub-title for this publication might be <u>Some Tentative Answers</u>
<u>to Questions Parents Ask</u>.

With these types of limitations in mind, I shall first state
the question commonly asked and then briefly outline the type of
answer usually formulated. It should be remembered that when
considering these answers, they may not really be appropriate for
the coordination problems of <u>your</u> child. Only a complete evaluation
on a child's total emotional, social, academic, perceptual and motor
abilities can truly serve his needs, and result in the answers to his
specific problems which are best rendered by professionals qualified
to diagnose and assess the various facets of his or her personality.

QUESTIONS AND ANSWERS

1. <u>Why is he this way? Why is he clumsy?</u>

There are numerous possible causes for minor to moderate movement
problems in children ranging from difficulties encountered at birth
to heredity, emotional maladjustment, and early childhood diseases.
Only your pediatrician can assign a reasonably accurate cause to his
problem, but it is sometimes not as helpful if the parent dwells
excessively on causes but rather looks carefully at the types of problems
seen, such as hand-eye coordination in writing, balance and agility
problems on the playground, running and walking awkwardly, and so forth,
and then formulates a program which is intended to remediate these
problems.

2. <u>My child reads well and is intelligent; why does he have coordination</u>
   <u>problems?</u>

The nervous system is extremely complex, and often children are
adequate or above average in verbal and reading comprehension and yet
have coordination problems. We work each year with children from a
school for the gifted who evidence motor development several years
below that expected for children their age. It is true, however, that
many clumsy children have difficulty expressing their intellect in
handwriting, etc., in finishing their math problems, in their spelling
lesson, and thus incoordination in writing provides a severe block
to the expression of their intellect.

While it is generally true that there are a greater percent of
children with coordination problems among groups of children with
learning problems including reading, there are children who are adroit

1. DEVELOPMENT

at games and yet have learning difficulties for a variety of reasons.
There is also a considerable amount of research in literature confirming
the fact that basic programs of movement activities will not necessarily
aid reading in either the poor reader or average reader.

3. <u>But can my child be made better? Can he be changed?</u>

Our research indicated that the children most likely to change
include those who are younger, from 2-6 years of age, as well as those
whose motor problems are less marked. Most likely to change are measures
of a child's fitness and strength; next liable to change are measures
of coordination, balance, agility, throwing and the like; in questionnaire
measures of the child's self-concept, collected by asking the child
questions of various kinds (i.e. "Are you the last to be chosen in
games?"), it is indicated that these feelings are more difficult to
modify quickly than are his physical performance scores.

4. <u>How long will it take to improve his coordination?</u>

Motor incoordination is not an infectious disease which is
checked via a quick inoculation of some kind of movement panacea.
We do not re-test children until they have been with us about six
months. When and if we change a child's motor competencies it is
not clear whether we modify some basic ingredient in his nervous
system or whether we simply aid him to develop more effective strategies
when performing motor skills such as standing with his feet further
apart when throwing, in the case of a balance problem, etc.

5. <u>What about little league, the program at the YMCA, and similar
youth programs?</u>

The primary principle to keep in mind is that exposing a clumsy
child to a program of physcial activity is likely <u>never</u> to have a
<u>neutral</u> effect upon his personality. It can be negative, indeed
devastating, or emotionally uplifting, depending upon the philosophy,
expertise, and patience of the instructor and the demands placed upon
the child for quick improvement. It is important that before placing
a child in such a program you, as a parent, observe the manner in
which the instructor works with children and also spend time asking
the instructor what he expects as well as telling him you child's
problem. If the instructor is too demanding, the program too "high
powered" with relationship to the demands for excellence, the child
with movement problems should be kept out ot it. On the other hand,
if the program is geared to the individual physical and emotional
needs of the children participating, incorporates basically sound

26

principles of teaching and learning, and contains adequate conditioning for strenuous activity, the child might be placed in it.

6. <u>What can I do with my child at home?</u>

Some parents can work with their own children in a program of remediation and some can not. If the child evidences problems of big muscle control, he might be given a program about three times a week (Monday-Wednesday-Friday) for an hour or less each time consisting of basic activities, including tumbling, balance beam work, some physical exercises, plus playground sport skills. The other days of the week (Tuesday-Thursday-Saturday) he might be given help with handwriting and printing.

There are several general principles to follow.

(a) Work on simple tasks at first such as jumping over a line in various ways, moving laterally backward, and the like, before going to more complex tasks like running and catching balls thrown from a distance.

(b) Keep the practice as free from emotional stress as possible; encourage, work within the child's capacities while attempting at times to help him to try to better his previously best efforts. Keep other children away who might ridicule his attempts at improvement.

(c) Work specifically on the areas of incompetence exhibited by the child; walking balance beams will help balance, not handwriting, for example. For help with the latter try practice in writing and printing using simple lead-up activities.

(d) Work both on basic activities such as agility, balance, and specific playground skills that the child states he needs. Ask "What are you doing in school now that I can help you with?" and then provide him with the activities he outlines.

(e) Provide a means following vigorous activity, through which the child can be aided to calm down. Relaxation training in which the child is placed in a comfortable position and then aided to alternately tighten and relax his muscles in response to your verbal commands, is a helpful activity, for example. Attempting to somehow drain off excess energy through vigorous physical activity when directed toward physically inept hyperactive youngsters is likely to have a negative effect; they are likely to become overaroused and too upset to even sleep that night following the program to which they have been exposed.

1. DEVELOPMENT

A simple home gymnasium can consist of a 2" x 4" board 10-15 feet long in the back yard, a few balls, and ropes and sticks to jump over. Most important is the creativity of the parent in utilizing these simple pieces of equipment. After closely directed activities are engaged in for a period of time ("Walk the balance beam as I show you"), children may be encouraged to demonstrate modifications of the activities to which they are exposed ("Jump over the line six different ways," or perhaps "Get from here to there four different ways.").

I have recently seen some marvelous examples of children who have been worked with by their parents, and have obviously been exposed to patience and kindness while being helped, and whose motor coordination has improved remarkably we.. On the other hand, you might seek special help, as the following answer indicates.

7. Where can I receive help with my child?

Hopefully, in the near future, all elementary and secondary schools will contain special remedial programs in which from 15-18% of the children in these schools who are likely to exhibit motor problems are given help. In the meantime, there are often programs at the local college or university; you might call the physical education departments or the departments of psychology or special education. Your calls may help initiate a program where none now exists, by demonstrating need. Sometimes a group of parents can get together, hire a physical education instructor or college student, and obtain materials and the help of professional consultants who might direct their efforts.

There are a number of self-styled perceptual-motor trainers in many communities today who may be evaluated using the following continuum. Do their credentials consist of mere interest, or do they have a background in education, special education, psychology and/or physical education? Do they promise to remediate all the child's educational and perceptual and emotional problems through motor activity? If they do, one should be extremely wary of working with them. Perhaps your pediatrician or school psychologist can recommend someone who is professionally qualified to engage in a physical education program specially suited to the needs of your child.

8. Won't he simply grow out of his coordination problems?

The child may or may not, in any case it is believed imperative if the child is younger to expose him to some attempt at remediation. We have viewed a number of children in late childhood who have been kept away from any early help, because of the "he'll grow out of it" philosophy. Usually, the emotional make-up seen in such children is extremely unstable, as they have received a number of years of social punishment from their peers by this time, and may also have incurred the censure of their teachers for failure to do their work in time.

9. <u>What can I do about the amount of special punishment heaped upon my child on the playground, because of his physical deficiencies?</u>

This is an extremely difficult problem. Most of the boys and girls we test report that their "friends make fun of them", and in other ways report ridicule directed toward them. Often an increase in skills elicits more favor from their classmates, but often even improvement in physical skill is not enough to overcome a reputation previously earned for clumsiness. Often a parent must remove a child from one school environment and place him in another, in order for him to exhibit his newly acquired physical skills.

Inordinate pressure from classroom teachers and/or physical education teachers for physical performance which the child is incapable of, should be "treated" by going to the teacher or principal and explaining the child's problem, if this is not effective, again he might be removed from the school, or a phone call from a professional worker (psychologist or physician) explaining the nature of the child's problem to the school official concerned might be helpful.

This type of social punishment is of course likely to compound the child's problem, and unless it is lessened is likely to lead to moderate to severe emotional problems. Without being overprotective, the parents should avail themselves of every means possible to prevent or lessen the impact or ridicule from other children or from school personnel. Fortunately, a great many school teachers and administrators in increasing numbers are sensitive observers of clumsy children and are instituting school programs to remediate this problem in the population for which they are responsible.

10. <u>Is this problem more prevalent in boys than in girls?</u>

Yes, it would seem so, and no one seems at this point to know the exact reasons why. At the same time it is becoming increasingly evident to us at UCLA that a clumsy girl often suffers the social problems for her physical ineptitude similar to those experienced by clumsy boys.

11. <u>May the better feelings which a child will engender about himself when improving his physical ability and acquiring success in games reflect in improved school work?</u>

Sometimes improved self-concept will result in more effort in school work by a child and sometimes not. At times low ability and motivation in games are part of a general syndrome of "effortlessness" seen in a number of areas, a syndrome which should be explored in depth by a child psychologist or child psychiatrist. At other times we have seen marked improvement in self-concept acquired because of improved physical ability which then results in improved work in school. At other times, a child's improvement in sports may not generalize and the child still may feel badly about his academic progress and remain a low achiever.

12. <u>What about special lessons in an individual sport, tennis or swimming, for example? Will accomplishment in these activities through extra tutoring help a child?</u>

If the instructor is patient, and the group pressures not great, this kind of experience can help a child gain self-confidence in himself through physical activity. Often these tutored games and activities are not those valued by their peers on the playground, and while swimming is an excellend conditioner and recreational activity, the transfer from swimming to other physical education activities seen on playgrounds is likely to be slight or absent.

13. <u>Will music lessons help or hinder a child?</u>

Again, if taught in a patient manner with little pressure, lessons in the piano, guitar, etc., may be helpful and enjoyable for a child with coordination problems. However, finger dexterity exercises, as seen in piano playing and guitar, etc., are not likely to help handwriting which employs a different type of coordination.

14. <u>How can I help my child's writing?</u>

Primarily by stress-free short practice sessions at home using various materials prepared for this purpose, a child's writing can be helped. At the same time, some older children with coordination problems, 10 and over, can be aided to express their intellect by teaching them to type. Although typing requires a different kind of coordination than the more fluid writing and printing tasks, at times a child may be more proficient in the former than in the latter.

If a child's printing is extremely erratic his hand may have to be guided, with the parent sitting behind the child, in the formation of his letters. When more proficiency is achieved, a cookie pan, with about 1/4th inch of modeling clay may be used to print in, thus the clay guides the point of the writing implement to some degree. Later the child can trace over letters, and finally he may be able to print without help or visual guides.

15. <u>What is easier, cursive handwriting or block printing? Which</u>
<u>should he try to do first?</u>

Many cursive letters, the "l's", "e's", and "i's", for example,
are similar to the early developmental stages in scribbling, and thus
are probably easier for most children than the stop and go motions needed
in printing. At the same time there are other written letters, most of
the capital letters, and those requiring cut-backs, such as "b", "d",
"q", "p", etc., which are probably more difficult for a child to exectue
than most of the printed letters. Cursive letters, or handwriting,
prevent the reversals some times seen when letters are printed.

16. <u>What about letter reversals when my child prints?</u>

Reversing letters, and the order of letters in words, is typical
of the normal five-year-old, just as the lack of accurate left-right
awareness at this age, is common. Almost one-half of all six-year-
olds will occasionally reverse letters. By the age of seven or eight,
however, this problem should disappear. Playing left-right games of
various kinds with the child may help, particularly if when seated in
front of letters and words, direct transfer instructions to the asym-
metries of words and letters are taught (for example: "See Johnny,
the rough part of the 'd' faces toward your left hand."). However,
the causes of poor reading are more complicated than simply reversal
problems, and clearing up reversal problems will not always result in
reading problems similarly disappearing.

17. <u>Just what should a child be able to do with his body at various</u>
<u>ages?</u>

A paperback text listed in your bibliography (5) contains
detailed guidelines. But, in general, by four years of age a normal
walking and running pattern should be seen in children, and they should
be able to walk 2" wide lines on the floor at this age without much
trouble. By four and five, a child should be able to catch a large
playground ball bounced to him from a short distance away, and should
hop on one foot and jump using both feet at the same time for a short
distance. If your child evidences problems executing these simple
tasks, and in drawing reasonably good circles and squares by the time he
enters school, it is possible that he is encountering some kind of
problem using his body in various ways, and should be thoroughly
evaluated by an educational psychologist and/or his doctor.

1. DEVELOPMENT

SUMMARY

Children with coordination difficulties are frequently found in so-called normal populations of children and consist primarily of boys. Remediation of their problems depends upon the age at which the problem is identified and the degree of dysfunction the child may evidence. Remedial measures should be properly sequenced, patiently applied, and encompass a broad range of activities directed toward the child's specific kinds of coordination problems.

Such children should not be subjected to inordinately stressful physical education or athletic programs in which performance is emphasized, within "emotionally charged conditions". Rather, they should be confronted with patiently applied physical activities in which they have some chance to do well. Handwriting and printing practice for short periods each day may result in imporvement, just as should programs in which fitness and the control of the larger muscles of the body are emphasized.

The research literature is clear in substantiating the fact that improvement in motor coordination will not necessarily result in improvement in various visual perceptual abilities, or in reading proficiency. At the same time, a child who may be failing beaause of a low self-concept caused by the social punishment of his peers because of lack of game proficiency may be helped in rather general ways by improving his coordination. Programs of remedial physical activities are important in achieving the goals inherent in the program, such as improving motor coordination without needing additional justification with reference to improvement in academic abilities.

A DEVELOPMENTAL APPROACH TO PERCEPTUAL-MOTOR EXPERIENCES

Dr. Marguerite Clifton
Purdue University,

Deriving sheer pleasure from mastery and use of one's body in executing all kinds of movement tasks should be a personal objective of all healthy individuals regardless of age. The physical and social dimensions of environments of the past and those unknown in centuries ahead continue to make varying demands on the human organism. Certainly not the least, but often the most neglected, is concern for man's ability to achieve satisfaction and self-confidence in encounters with the dimensions of his personal physcial and social environment. Too often, attention to the physical aspect of man is rationalized only for its contribution to his cognitive function.

Although high premium is placed on cognitive excellence, a dichotomy seems to exist for our culture which also places a high premium on man's excellence in the use of his body through superior performance in popular cultural movement forms such as football, basketball, dance, and golf, to name but a few examples. Pressure to excel, in whatever the form. begins early. Complex sports forms long ago invaded the world of the elementary age child in our culture, chiefly involving boys, but seldom girls. The pressure for a child to compete with others in various activities, whether he wishes to or not, is not necessarily evil. This can be a positive type of experience among many which enables a child to say "I can do it." It offers him opportunities to develop realistic self-concepts of his performance in each of many different domains. Exposure to many kinds of experience can, with adequate guidance, help the child achieve increasing congruence between his "real" self and his "ideal" self—a notable objective for continuing emotional stability.

We must ask ourselves, however, are we providing *all* children with a head start on their early confrontation with potentially ego-shaking situations requiring one's best use of his body in movement tasks? Perhaps not. Parental attention in late infancy and early childhood is given over primarily to proper nutrition, rest, toilet training, and cognitive development particularly in terms of language skills. Meanwhile, the young child usually approaches physical tasks without special attention or guidance. In many instances, he is actually inhibited, if not temporarily retarded, by adults transporting him, harassed mothers confining him to a restricting play pen, parental discouragement of his exploratory movement (the furnishings are too precious), and a host of other acts that "save" the parent but limit the child's movement repertoire.

The nursery school has been with us for many decades and has encompassed many changes so preschool educational experience prior to kindergarten is not new. However, the institution of Head Start programs, funded by the federal government, has called even greater attention to the necessity of early intervention to foster enhancement of cognitive development. The child development and educational psychology literature fairly abounds in recent years with reports of research on programs of early education, some beginning with early infancy. Increased interest is also apparent from studies regarding behavior *in utero* and effects on later cognitive development.

Many programs for young children are specifically directed toward individuals with learning difficulties. These range from conditions of the severely retarded to children experiencing some reading difficulty. Many of these programs are benefited by the physical educator and his knowledge of movement behavior. We should indeed be proud of our increasing contribution to children participating in programs of special education.

Physical educators and child development specialists over the years have garnered considerable research evidence regarding the status of motor development, infancy through adulthood. Performance norms established in the 1920's, '30's, and '40's are still used as standards for assessing readiness levels—"to hop," "to throw," "to catch." However, increased attention to Piaget's theory of learning, new minitheories about perceptual input, and a shift in the sociocultural climate concerning early learning strongly suggest that physical educators should give concerted effort to maximizing the child's opportunities for early sensory stimulation accompanied by gradual self-application of principles in executing a variety of movement tasks.

A long-term developmental movement education program for children ages two to five, offering community service and acquisition of longitudinal information, has been initiated by the Department of Physical Education for Women at Purdue University. Many obvious benefits can be derived by participating families. Other benefits no less important are in turn received by the sponsoring department. A few of these include: early teaching experience for major students; a live laboratory setting for students to observe the practical application of principles that are discussed in lectures; student and faculty involvement in research directly related to movement dimensions studied in the undergraduate curriculum; collection of longitudinal data concerning development and performance of specific movement tasks; and not least important, an opportunity to bring "town and gown" closer to an operation of mutual concern.

1. DEVELOPMENT

Organization

An 11-week, one day per week, pilot program involving 39 children preceded the organization and implementation of the developmental movement education program. Perhaps in the near future, three or four units will be in operation, each aimed at a different age population or development of a highly specific movement product.

Meanwhile, the current program is designed for boys and girls ages 24 months through 66 months. The session that ended in December 1969 included 35 boys, 35 girls, 9 faculty, and 62 undergraduate students. The program model is one ten-week session each semester. Each child participates two days a week in two-hour periods each day. The teacher-child ratio is as follows: age two: one teacher to one child; age three: one teacher to one child (50%) and one teacher to two children (50%); age four: one teacher to three children; age five: one teacher to three children. Following initial minor adjustments, one of the major procedural objectives is providing the child with the same teacher throughout the ten weeks. This is a fee structured program supported by parents and without benefit of agency funding for direct operation.

Purposes

The program philosophy, selection of areas of experience, the nature of behavioral objectives, program interpretation, the nature of progress reports, the direction of research, and the procedures for selecting program participants are guided by the following assumption and hypotheses:

Assumption
Early and systematic stimulation of senses critical to perceptual-motor functioning and emphasis on developmental pacing enables the child to operate effectively in a variety of movement experiences.

Hypotheses
1. Children will perform specific motor tasks with greater efficiency after each 20-session program.
2. Children will increase their accuracy in self-prediction of performance on both familiar tasks and related, but unfamiliar tasks.
3. Children will exhibit increased positive attitudes toward performing the motor tasks in the three areas included in the program.
4. Parents will increase their positive attitudes toward provision of vigorous physical activity for both boys and girls.

AQUATIC AREA

Objectives

1. To foster the achievement of ease and self-confidence in the water through individually planned experiences tailored to each child's departure point and progress through the program.
2. To improve performance, as directed toward four areas:
   adjustment, buoyancy and balance skills
   propulsion skills
   face in the water and breathing skills
   entry skills

Organization

Similar age children are in the pool together, each with his own instructor in a one to one ratio. The length of time in the water ranges from 20 minutes for two-year olds to 40 minutes for five-year olds. Prior experience beyond "bath tub splashing" varies considerably. Over half of the children, however, usually have not had experience in some body of water be it pool, lake, or ocean.

Flotation devices of any kind are seldom used. Thus, the environment requires the child to rely on the use of his own body in order to stay afloat. One of the real difficulties sometimes encountered is occasioned by the children whose parents have used flotation supports on the child when at the lake or beach. Generally, this child takes a longer time to orient himself to the pool experience.

A sequential list of potential experiences arranged within the aquatic objectives cited above provides teachers with an array of choices for use with each youngster depending on his individual progress and occasional remissions. Availability of a poolside record keeping system enables teachers to record specific behavior information at the conclusion of one time block and review the progress record of the next child before he enters the pool area.

IN-SERVICE EDUCATION

In-service education is an important aspect, and each semester of experience with the program indicates a need for more workshops for students and faculty. A handbook developed by the faculty involved provides teacher-students and volunteers with a basic reference, in addition to which they receive other materials, readings, and films for viewing.

Increased parent understanding and appreciation for movement in developmental experiences is accomplished in numerous ways: (1) preregistration literature generally explaining the program, (2) program orientation, (3) group discussion spaced throughout the 10-week session, (4) daily observation of own child during participation, (5) teacher-parent conference as needed, (6) summary of progress session, and (7) written participation in program evaluation.

The need for early sensory stimulation applicable to motor performance is well documented and discussed elsewhere in this feature issue. Thus, this program represents a systematic attempt by university physical educators to "close the gap" between theoretical study in the university and action programs in the community and school environment.

Transporting young children to the university setting, as employed in this program, is not necessarily the ideal to be sought. These initial efforts, however, may lead to the eventual establishment of minischools throughout the community, thus reaching a wider range of children. Professionals and university educated paraprofessionals from the community would work as a team to accomplish objectives similar to those ascribed to the present program. Research studies conducted cooperatively by professionals, paraprofessionals, and interested parents would, it is hoped, yield evidence on a continuing basis which would provide supportable rationale for action programs in developmental movement education.

MANAGEMENT FOR LEARNING THROUGH MOVEMENT

Betty M. Flinchum, Ph.D.

Professor of Education, University of North Florida,
Jacksonville, Florida

PLANNING THE ENVIRONMENT

The components of movement according to development facts should be the basis for the selection of a movement-learning environment for a particular age level. Recognizing that all children do not grow and develop at the same rate, the individual basis within each learning session should provide a comprehensive range of movement patterns. No child should be subjected to planned, rigid movement patterns, with the expectations of achievement precluded. Good planning procedure will provide for the challenge and interest of all children. A well-organized play area can challenge each child, and offer enjoyable physical rewards for all. Achieving objectives can be assured.

Let us think in terms of motor development progression from infancy. The child first learns to grasp, to climb, to crawl, and to walk. These stages are fairly well established, but each child will not achieve these stages at the same age. It has been known that learning takes place in the situation where the development of any skill is commensurate with the individual's ability. Although games are based on the basic skills, they are structured, patterned movements that a child must master in order to excel. Children who have had very little previous exposure to skill acquisition, or who may be handicapped in some respect, are penalized. Therefore, it is important to include all the children in the activities. Very young children do not need structured movement sessions.

Fundamental motor skills relate to all live activities, not just games. Experience has shown that when children have a chance at physical activity, without group pressure, participation is a joy, and management is less of a burden.

ORGANIZING THE LEARNING ENVIRONMENT

Children should be dressed for activity so that movement is not inhibited. This can be achieved with a minimum of effort. With parental support, children can be dressed appropriately on coming to the sessions. Happily, many children now dress for mobility. Shoes may be removed

1. DEVELOPMENT

for better freedom and to enhance tactile input.

The program outlined for the preschool will be based on the use of equipment, and basic movement leading to overall motor development. In this program, each child must have his own space and equipment.

The use of the equipment will encourage the child to explore and to improve the progress individually; to gain eye-hand coordination skills with balloons, balls, with paddles and balls, bats and balls; to handle the body in relation to objects; and above all, to understand the body, how it moves—what it can do. The child will be building a vocabulary of movements, and will be moving, growing, and learning to adjust to this growth.

SAFETY

The hazards of play often tend to limit the liberties which teachers allow in movement lessons. One factor that should be considered is that *children will only attempt those feats in which they feel confident.* It follows, therefore, that in using the problem-solving technique, the child will provide his own limits. *Under no circumstances* should the teacher suggest *danger* to the child. Inspire confidence by giving encouragement for a daring performance.

The teacher *can* contribute to the safety of the lesson by being observant toward play area hazards. The area should be carefully inspected before each lesson, and all possible danger spots eliminated. Equipment should be inspected for breaks or splinters. Making a safe area is a very important part of the lesson planning.

The teacher should also be aware of each child's movements at all times during the lessons. Proper organization and control is essential to good movement training.

ORGANIZATIONAL CHECKLIST FOR MOVEMENT LESSON

1. Prepare review of previous lesson (such as a story).
2. Prepare daily objectives for proposed lesson.
3. Agree on a control signal with children (such as freeze).
4. Prepare alternate lesson for inclement weather (only where necessary).
5. Plan for utilization of space and learning centers.
6. Diagram area with marking and targets needed.
7. Plan for all needed equipment. (Be sure each child has equipment.)
8. Plan for equipment improvisation (where necessary).
9. Place equipment in area preceding arrival of children.
10. Make safety check.
11. Plan for activities to change with least possible confusion.
12. Arrange for helpers to bring in equipment and work with children.
13. Prepare a task for immediate absorption on arrival.
14. Plan how to get pupils to and from the play area.

FLOOR PLAN

In preparation for a movement lesson, make learning centers in the play space. This will situate each child 3 to 5 feet away from other children on all sides, and will provide him with plenty of space for exploring his own abilities. When the children enter the learning environment, allow each child to find a learning center and begin to explore. For the first several weeks it may be necessary to continually reinforce the importance of each child using his own learning center and apparatus.

The children should soon learn to relate to their space as a center of orientation, and around this idea the activities described in this chapter can be organized.

A definite value of this type of organization is that it gives opportunity for large or small group work. Once the different motor learning centers have been determined by the teacher, it is then possible to deal with challenges in individual ways.

The floor plan demonstrates how certain areas of the movement space can be used to work on different problem levels. One area can be used for balance work or mat work involving locomotion. Another area can be used for perceptual problems involving the tracking skills or eye-hand coordination. The remainder of the class can participate in various activities using the space for locomotor relationships.

MOVEMENT CENTERS
Indoor spaces

An indoor space for movement should be set up in an area where the child can enjoy it freely. It should contain equipment for eye-hand coordination and environmental stimuli such as balls and targets, fleece balls, goals, walls for rebounds and catching skills, beanbags, hoops and ropes, suspended balls, bats, and other manipulative objects. It should also include mats, climbing ropes, balance equipment, portable climbing equipment such as blocks and ladders, mirrors for children to observe their own movements, cubes, tubes, and other perceptually challenging equipment. All the equipment in the space should provide sensorimotor stimuli,

Fig. 8-1

that is, different textures, geometric designs, sound equipment, colors, and other stimulating motivators for purposeful action.

Outdoor space

Outdoor play space has often been designed to amuse chidlren, rather than to provide motor development learning experiences. Properly designed outdoor play centers should provide space to run freely with up and down hillsides and challenging obstacles for dodging and climbing over. Portable obstacles are preferred to fixed ones to enable the child to redesign the areas. Portable boxes, ladders, barrels, and planks will challenge creativity and child-centered design. Smooth, hard surfaces are essential to offer spaces to ride or push wheeled equipment and for bouncing balls. The hard surfaces should have adjacent flat walls for use with balls and paddles. Lines and targets in different colors may be painted on the hard surfaces.

Climbing, hanging, and crawling equipment should be installed on grassy areas and around the edges of the open spaces. A trampoline-like piece of equipment made from an old bed spring may be set up as a jumping pit in this area. Sand boxes, wading pools, and other small group activity centers may be added.

Trees are essential for climbing and for shade areas. They also provide a place for the child to sit and to observe the activities of other children from a different perspective.

Outdoor spaces can be very creatively designed to allow for flexibility of arrangement, especially if very few obstacles and equipment are fixed. Swings, slides, fixed "jungle gyms," and rocking horses are not recommended since they "move the children" rather than allowing the children to move themselves.

SPECIFIC EQUIPMENT: INDOOR-OUTDOOR
Equipment

Equipment for use in an early childhood movement education program can be made. Since large apparatus is the most expensive when purchased, methods of construction of indoor apparatus and a creative outdoor play are suggested. These ideas may serve as a motivator to creativity in developing one's own equipment.

Larger equipment

Climbing stairs—movable but not too steep
Rocking boat-stairs combination
Balance boards—2 × 4 inches × 10 feet with reversible bases
Planks and trestles (aluminum preferred)
Trampoline, innerspring mattress, large inner tubes covered with canvas
Climbing ropes, cargo nets
Wall targets, supended targets
Rebound throwing nets
Wooden blocks—12 × 12 × 12 inches, 4 × 4 × 12 inches, 24 × 8 × 8 inches
Variable speed phonograph (tempo control)
Tumbling mats or lightweight mattress
Plastic wading pool, sand box, jumping pits
Cardboard boxes
Percussion instruments

Movable saw horses
Movable planks and blocks
Push and pull objects
Ladders
Movable horizontal bars
Tunnels, boxes
Tires (various sizes)
Spools
Rubber utility balls
Plastic whiffle balls, baseball size
Plastic whiffle balls, softball size
Yarn balls, various sizes
Short plastic bats
Sponge rubber ball, 3 inch diameter, or used tennis balls
Frisbees (or sturdy paper plates)
Balloons
Beach balls
Hula hoops
Jump ropes
Chinese stretch ropes
1 inch wide flat strips of rubber tubes
Plastic detergent bottles (scoops)
Drum
Tambourine
Bamboo poles, various sizes from 3 to 8 feet long
Phonograph records
Wands of different colors
Milk cartons
Suspended balls
Walking beams, round and square

HOW TO MAKE SMALL APPARATUS EQUIPMENT
Hoops (Fig. 8-2)

Hoops for young children can be made from small garden hose ⅛ inch in diameter. Hose lengths may vary according to the age of the child:

Fig. 8-2

lengths of 24 to 30 inches are successful for preschool ages. The hose is cut and ends are joined with a dowel and stapled (tape should be used to cover the staples). It may be possible to join the ends over the dowel and have it hold without the use of the staples.

Large hoops can be made by cutting ¾-inch pipe into lengths 8⅓ feet long, fastening the ends together with dowel and heavy duty staples. This joint is then covered with electricians' tape.

Small hoops can be made from ⅜ inch garden hose cut into lengths of 54 inches and joined together with a 1½ inch piece of ⅜ inch dowel. Tape joining point.

Ring-toss hoops can be made the same way but cut into shorter lengths. Tape the joined edges.

Ring-toss target can be made using 1 inch thick board. Almost any size square can be used. Nail a 5½ or 6 inch piece of ¾ inch dowel to the center of the square, then paint (Fig. 8-3).

Tire maze

A series of tires are placed in the ground at varied heights and at different angles. The children walk on top of the tires, go over them in different ways, or crawl through them.

Balls

Preschool children start eye-hand activity with balloons or fleece or yarn balls. When the child progresses to playground balls, the 6- or 7-

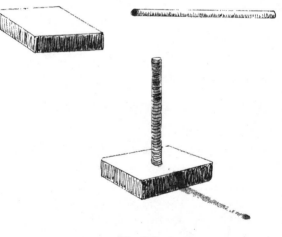

Fig. 8-3

inch ball is the easiest for this age to handle. It is important to expose the children to different size balls.

During the final phases of the movement program in preschool, children should be exposed to activity with basketballs, volleyballs, kickballs, and suspended balls. These are not the most important, however, and should not be purchased until other equipment is secured. These balls can often be obtained from the upper elementary physical education teachers.

The plastic ball in either softball or baseball size is a very usable item. These balls can be easily converted into suspended balls by tying sash cord through the holes. Tape should be used to reinforce the tying space.

Yarn balls (Fig. 8-4)

Place two cardboard circles with hole in the center, one on top of the other, and wind the yarn around cardboard, cut around edge, wrap and tie between cardboard, then cut and remove cardboard.

Another way to make a yarn ball is to cut a piece of cardboard approximately 4 inches long and about 2 inches wide. Wrap the yarn around the long side of the cardboard until it appears full. Slip the yarn off the cardboard and tie a piece of yarn around the center. Cut the looped ends and fluff.

Fig. 8-4

Beanbags (Fig. 8-5)

Cut material of different textures into various sizes and shapes, sew edges and fill with dried beans or corn, and close openings. Embroider numbers or letters on the outside of the bag after it is finished.

Scoops (Fig. 8-6)

Using empty, cleaned out bleach bottles, preferably ½- or 1-gallon bottles, cut the portion as shown and tape the edges.

Targets (Fig. 8-7)

Use cans. After they have been open and cleaned out, paint them different colors. When the paint has dried, tape the opened edge. They could also be numbered or lettered. They can be stacked and used as targets.

Fig. 8-5
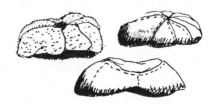

1. DEVELOPMENT

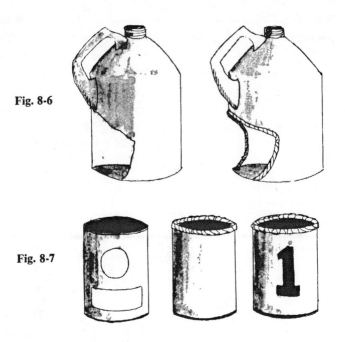

Fig. 8-6

Fig. 8-7

Cup-ball game (Fig. 8-8)

For handle cut dowel stick into 5-inch lengths. Tack a plastic cup onto the handle but before you tack on completely, tie a piece of string or yarn around the tack, then tack together completely. Glue or use a needle to attach a small ball or fishing cork. The handles and balls can be painted.

Teetering boards (Fig. 8-9)

You need a block of wood that is 12 × 12 inches and you glue a half circle to the bottom of the block. When the glue has dried, also paint this one to make it more interesting for the children.

Fig. 8-8

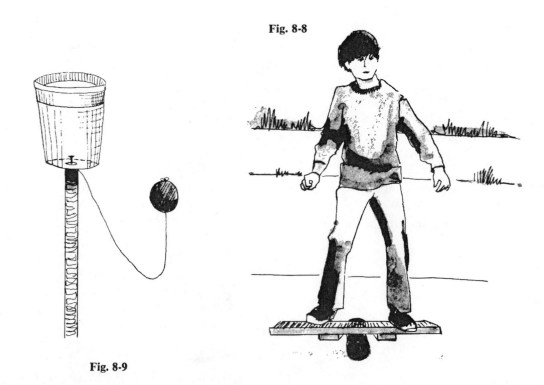

Fig. 8-9

Ropes (Fig. 8-10)

The ropes are made by obtaining pieces of rope (the strength and texture to one's taste) and cutting them into an appropriate length, binding the raw edges with tape, so that they won't ravel. The tape also provides the children with a type of handle for holding.

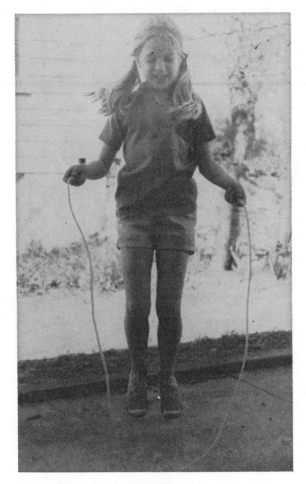

Fig. 8-10

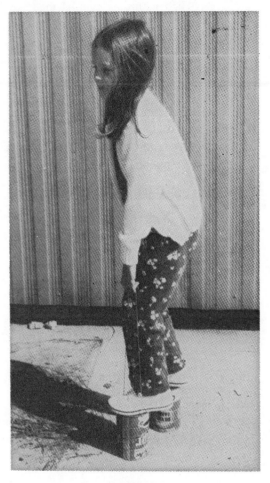

Fig. 8-11

Stilts (Fig. 8-11)

The tin can stilts are made by obtaining some large cans (such as those for juice) and removing the label. Tape around the edges to prevent the child from getting cut. Drill holes on opposite sides of the can and thread the rope through the can. Knot and then bind with tape to prevent it from coming apart. Paint may now be applied to the can and the stilts are ready to use.

Climber (Fig. 8-12)

This piece of equipment is made from two saw horse type pieces with three cross bars in a line. These bars are drilled with holes into which several types of equipment may be fastened between the two. These include 4- by 4-inch beams, walking boards, spring boards, and parallel bars. Many variations are possible.

1. DEVELOPMENT

Hurdles (Fig. 8-13)

A simple way to make hurdles is to use cardboard boxes and yard-sticks. Jump ropes may also be tied between traffic cones. A more versatile hurdle is made by drilling ½-inch holes at 8-inch intervals along a 4- by 4-inch board. The board is then cut into sections through the center of the holes. One-quarter inch dowels, 3 feet in length, are used for crossbars. Higher hurdles may be made by stacking. Two dowels may be used with four blocks to make a window effect for going through.

Tunnels (Fig. 8-14)

Tunnels can be constructed by bolting tires together and setting them in cement. Children may go over or through tunnels or they may jump from tunnel to tunnel.

Indoor-outdoor tunnels may be made from 55-gallon drums with both ends removed. Two are placed in frames at different heights and two are placed end to end in a low frame for a long tunnel.

Vertical ladder (Fig. 8-15)

Make the ladder in varied heights with varying distance between rungs.

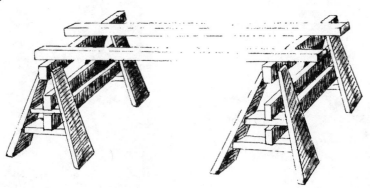

Fig. 8-12

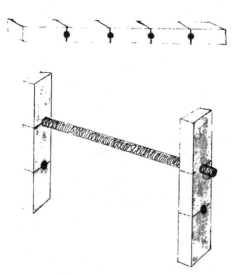

Fig. 8-13

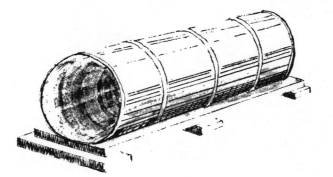

Fig. 8-14

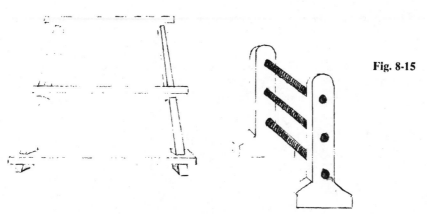

Fig. 8-15

Spinner

Cable spools are supported so that they may spin freely. Children try to walk on top of these or simply to balance in any way on them.

Spools

Various size cable spools are set in the ground at varied heights. The children move from spool to spool without touching. Different size spools are used so that children must control their bodies on different size areas while changing levels.

Towers

A series of cable spools are bolted together to form towers of various heights. The child may climb from tower to tower, jump from tower to tower, or from the towers to the ground.

Climbing apparatus

Supported from a tree, two ropes, a rope ladder, and a climbing pole are available for the children to use.

Climbing nets

The child experiences a sensation of free moving in all directions while climbing the net. Commercially built nets are available in several sizes.

Grip travel

An old swing set has been modified to support grip devices made from the ends of baseball bats.

Traveling rings

A 2- by 4-inch board is fastened between two trees. Traveling rings are supported from this.

1. DEVELOPMENT

Traveling tires

Small car tires are hung from a limb that is parallel to the ground. The children climb into, through, and from tire to tire.

Balance beams (Fig. 8-16)

The balance beam is the standard equipment in this area. Rather than use the commercial beam that is adjustable to a 2- or 4-inch width it is more satisfactory to construct longer boards that are set permanently. By

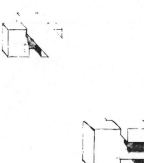

Fig. 8-16

using stools, balance beams may be raised to different heights. In addition, a more challenging course can be developed by using inclined, angled, and tapered beams.

Balance benches (Fig. 8-17)

The benches are constructed from 1- by 6-inch stock 8 feet in length. Benches both 10 inches and 20 inches high are used. The bench also has a 2-inch balance beam when turned upside down. The center supports are used to step through when the bench is laid on its side. The benches may be bolted together in a step pattern or "log cabin" design.

Used with the vertical ladders, inclines of different angles may be set up as well as setting the bench up to 3 feet off the ground.

Individual mats

If all children are to work on balance activities at the same time, it is important to have individual mats. A heavy rug may be cut into sections 3 by 4 feet and serve well for this purpose. Some sections both larger and smaller may be cut to add variety in work space.

Rocking boards, teeter boards, and roller-rollers

These are used both separately and with ball activities. The children also may work individually or in groups.

Tire patterns

Both car tires and bicycle tires are used to set patterns on the floor. The child can be given specific directions in using the patterns that require balance on either one or both feet or on some other part of the body.

Fig. 8-17

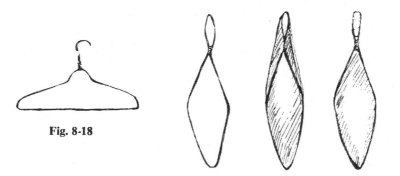

Fig. 8-18

Trampolines

Not the trampoline as usually thought of but rather large inner tubes either placed on mats or used on the grass is the trampoline of the kindergarten level. In addition, bounce boards may be constructed from 1- by 6-inch stock fastened to rounded 4- by 4-inch or 2- by 4-inch boards.

Fig. 8-19

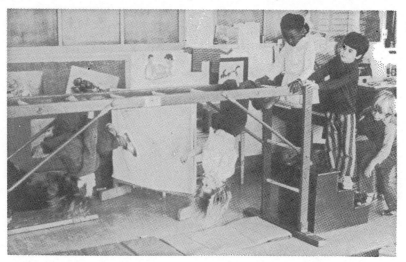

1. DEVELOPMENT

Horses

Horses are primarily used to help pupils with upside-down balance. Horses are very useful but are time-consuming and fairly expensive to construct.

Targets

Targets should be meaningful to the child. Animal faces and clown faces are popular. Colors, shapes, and suspended targets are also well liked by small children.

Bats (Fig. 8-18)

A safe and inexpensive bat may be made for kindergarten children by bending a coat hanger into the desired shape and covering it with an old stocking, taping the handle and edges. Different color tape may be used. Support hose offers great resiliency.

Small yarn balls may be made for use with the bats or fleece balls, or may be purchased. Fleece balls are commercially prepared, but can be easily made.

A PERSPECTIVE ON EDUCATION

Ray H. Barsch

> *Man considered not merely as an organized being but as a rational agent and a member of society is perhaps the most wonderfully contrived and to us the most interesting specimen of Divine wisdom that we have any knowledge of.*
>
> Whately

The concept of explorations into outer space by manned space vehicles capable of rendezvous, landing on other planets and advancing man's knowledge of the Universe has passed from the pages of science fiction to science reality in the short span of little more than a decade. The imagination of an entire world has been captivated by the exploits of the astronauts and the cosmonauts. Another frontier of ignorance is giving way to man's irrepressible desire to know his universe and understand his relationship to it. Historians have already christened this era in mankind's time as the Age of Space and every school child has incorporated a wide assortment of "space" terms into his everyday vocabulary.

Space exploration is another miracle of modern science. Remarkable as these astronautic adventures may be from a scientific viewpoint they are surpassed by the prosaic daily miracle of the newborn infant's conquest of terrestrial space.

While the collective genius of man combined to achieve the technological advances necessary to explore "outer space" and claim it's conquest, the world of "inner space" has always been his domain.

Every infant born can be considered a "terranaut" automatically receiving such a commission as a human birthright. His exploits in space will rival those of the astronauts in comparative complexity. In his exploration of terrestrial space each child will conquer the spatial mysteries of climbing stairs, running uphill, pedaling a bicycle, batting a ball, skating on blades or wheels, writing his name, drawing a form and will resolve thousands of other spatial dilemmas. Each "terranaut" leads an extremely busy exploratory existence. He moves to seek objects, transports objects from one place to another, experiments with height, depth and width, circumvents obstacles———moving through learning the greater is their explorative proficiency. Each infant terranaut explores his world in preparation for his preschool advancements which lead him to his elementary and secondary years of exploration and then onward to his vocational, marital, social, economic and citizen explorations. The journey from infancy to seniority passes through many worlds of space. The ease with which it is accomplished by most youngsters is a credit to the basic design of the "capsule" and the manner in which each one is programmed for transport. The human organism is designed for efficiency. The Great Architect conceived a remarkable being. The manner in which that design is dynamically expressed from infancy through adulthood constitutes the concern of this book.

Three major terrains of space must be travelled by every terranaut—(1) the Primary terrain mapped out from infancy to his entry into the second major locale of (2) Academic space bounded by the markers of elementary, secondary and collegiate schooling in preparation for his lengthy journey on the terrain of (3) Adulthood.

The Primary Terrain

The infancy period of man is devoted to the establishment of those patterns of cognitive and physical movements which will support a lifetime of adaptation—to teach the organism the rules and regulations governing "human beingness." The new organism is provided with a dual guide system in the form of a mother and father. Both parties having reached adulthood are presumed by biologic maturity to be prepared to act as guides in teaching the "lessons of the world" to the neophyte. In the earliest organization of the family unit the task of the parent was to prepare the offspring to eventually assume an adult role in the existing society. Whatever the tribal rules may have been according to geography, religion, economics and so on the obligation of the parent in primitive society as well as modern Space Age society has always been the same — to transmit the culture.

Sears (1957) has described the parents of America as the "conveyor belts of society" developing a product to enter the socio-economic stream of our nation. While a small percentage of the nation's parents may legitimately be accused of neglect, rejection and deliberate negative influence the vast majority of our parents try to do the best possible job of rearing their children.

Behavioral scientists have accumulated a significant list of what might generally be termed "the wrong things to do to a child", but this effort has not been matched by an equal amount of investigation on the topic of the "right things to do to a child". This listing of "rights" must usually be inferred from the listing of "wrongs." It is safe at this time to state that an appropriate child-rearing curriculum has not been defined. There is evidence from the Sears (1957) study on child-rearing practices among parents of normal children and the Barsch (1967) study on child-rearing practices among the parents of handicapped children which indicates that the average parent tends to rely upon a trial and error approach to rearing a child as a primary method followed in second place by parental models, i.e., the way their own parents reared them, and in third place, to be guided by "peer example", i.e., utilizing the same techniques as the "lady next door." Most parents probably rely upon all three approaches at one time or another.

As a consequence of this rather random process, there is probably relatively little understanding of what constitutes an appropriate set of life experiences during the first five years of life to guarantee that a child will arrive at the kindergarten doorstep experientially prepared according to the desires of the educational system. Preschool and kindergarten teachers will quickly attest to the shaping process which they must undertake to convert a youngster into a pupil. No adequate system of preparing a child for school has as yet been communicated to the parents of our nation. In general we seem to rely upon faith in the average parent to provide a suitable five year period of basic training for an academic career.

The vast majority of our nation's parents have a dedicated interest to rearing their children for achievement in school. Every parent hopes his child will sail smoothly and safely on academic seas. The multiplicity of experiences and activities required to ensure a successful voyage must be delineated to guide parents in their task.

The infancy and preschool period may be characterized as a truly remarkable period in the Ages of Man. Within this four to five year period the human organism constructs a physical and cognitive experiential foundation for movement efficiency which will serve him throughout a lifetime. Through movement and exercise he acquires sufficient strength of muscle to support his own weight and to push, pull and lift within the limits of his total size. He learns to move in balance using both sides of his body as reciprocally interweaving halves to jump, run, skip, kneel, crawl, roll and ride a tricycle. He becomes aware of his own body parts and the nature of their relationship one to another as well as achieving a recognition of how each part may serve him in his personal adaptation to the world in which he lives. Within that period of time he acquires a basic orientation of his own position in space in relation to all other objects which he might encounter. He achieves some recognition of time and its relation to him in terms of his rewards, goals and desires. He learns to see in order that he might see to learn. He learns to hear so that he might listen to learn. He learns to talk in order that he might express in communication with others the uniqueness of his own "beingness". He learns to move his body parts so that he may move efficiently to secure the information he needs. He learns to touch so that he may learn from contact with his world. He develops his sensitivity to smell so it may serve him in the discrimination of the attractive and unattractive odors in his world.

He acquires grace and ease in his movements and progressively becomes more rhythmic. He tries to utilize both sides of his body to acquire a proficiency at manipulation. In the bitter laboratory of early childhood he learns that all events cannot occur exactly as he may desire and acquires some form of response to disappointment. He learns to plan his moves to strategically achieve his intended goal progressively becoming more adept at circumventing and avoiding obstacles. Washing hands, bathing, dressing, throwing a ball, building blocks, winding a toy, dancing to rollicking records, talking to friends, talking to strangers, going for a walk, visiting grandma, planning a birthday — the list of learnings and accomplishments are endless.

Each achievement advances his proficiency as a traveler in terrestrial space. The canvas of development is the working surface.

Development paints a dynamic portrait of a man, plotting an organization of space, sketching in crude pencil lines the earliest outline of a particular detail and then progressively, adds body and depth with shading and nuances to evoke its proper relationship to all other portions of the portrait—it builds in perspective through time and eventually fills in the space.

Securing his development and insuring his readiness to cope with the multiplicity of problems which are yet to confront him in the next sixty to seventy years—his parents stand by enlisted in the service of his development giving active help when needed, quietly observing his independent struggles to achieve mastery and wisely noting the time for adult intervention versus the time to allow for independent exploration. Through it all he is moving. From birth to year one and to each succeeding birthday he is moving bit by bit toward the complexity of adulthood. Each advancement serving only as an introduction to some more complicated learning which must follow to fulfill his commitment to adulthood.

The societal obligation of the parent is to establish, define and structure the basic rules of living. Most parents address themselves to this task with a sincere dedicated effort. In the light of their effort, most parents feel reasonably confident that they have achieved a proper preparation of their offspring by the time he reaches kindergarten age. It has become a comfortable pastime among diagnosticians to point an accusing finger at the parent for some omission in the child-rearing procedure when a child reaches a point of failure during elementary years. Since there is common agreement on the importance of the learning in those first five years and since the parent is the natural party of responsibility the diagnosis of a child problem which defies explanation on physical or intellectual grounds leads inevitably to a search for parental omissions to account for the current situation. The evidence is too overwhelming to deny that such an accusation is frequently justified. While it is perhaps possible in the orientation of some clinicians to achieve such an explanation even though the psychological "fit" is difficult the possibility of explaining some of the failure patterns experienced by children on other bases than psychologic dysfunction of parents must certainly be considered.

Few parents are aware that they have borne a "terranaut"—an explorer of space. They discover it when he moves into forbidden places, climbs to dangerous heights, insists on experimenting and must "have his fingers into everything" but rarely do they attribute such exploration to a search for spatial orientation. Many well-intended parents fail to help a child acquire a system for building generalizations of space and building new concepts of space.

Most parents find that their little terranaut tends to conform to the expected standards learning to walk, talk, feed, dress, bathe and run according to the norms. A certain percentage of parents will face the problem of rearing a child whose development does not conform to expected standards for various reasons. These special children eventually receive a label to designate their developmental problem. The little terranauts whose fledgling explorations are complicated by physical, neurologic, emotional or sensory impairments have their own special problems in establishing a spatial proficiency on which to build a lifetime of progressive complexity. Their parents require a special awareness and assistance in guiding their child-rearing practices. The special child is no less a space explorer than the unimpaired child. The commitment of the parent is not reduced. The lessons of life must still be taught. The infancy and early childhood of the terranaut deserves a spatial perspective from both research and practice if the journey into other life spaces is to be made comfortably and expeditiously. Biology provides the launching pad and the parents provide the original directional guidance system. Their briefing for their mission must therefore inform them of the full and abiding nature of the traveler born into their charge.

The School Period

It is the customary practice in our American society to register the five year old for enrollment in the kindergarten of his neighborhood school to initiate the formal process of instruction leading to graduation as an intelligent, contributing, vocationally successful, economically independent, emotionally mature, socially adaptive, and politically sensitive and concerned member of society. For most children the kindergarten year represents an introduction to a form of group experience which they have never before encountered. In their own families they have associated with siblings of varying ages, either more mature or less than they. They may have spent happy hours playing with neighborhood children of the same age. But it is unlikely that they have experienced a group of 25-35 boys and girls of their own age in the same setting involved in the same activity.

The kindergarten year is the first full test for the terranaut. For the first time in a very real way he or she is asked to demonstrate in a peer-comparison setting the results of his five year program of basic training. All of the lessons of basic motor performance, oral language structure, form perception, color discrimination, independent toileting and dressing, "sharingness", conformity to patterns, ability to follow auditory and visual directions and many, many more functions in a seemingly endless list are expected to be properly organized, defined and integrated. According to the general rules of his society he has now moved into the social institution of a school to enter the next significant stage of preparation for adulthood. From the day he releases his mother s hand to greet the lady whom he will come to call "my teacher" until the time some thirteen years later when he is photographed in cap and gown proudly clutching a high school diploma approximately one third of all of his waking hours will be devoted to school. From September to June each of the thirteen years he will be "employed" for approximately six to seven hours per day five days per week. His schedule will be regular and his "off" days are carefully defined. His occupation can be listed as an "apprentice citizen."

During that space he will become familiar with all previous explorations of man delving into the history of man, cultural developments, basic fundamentals of all sciences, great literature, mathematical systems—all systematized and attractively packaged for his consumption by those who have gone before. He will cognitively explore man's past, evaluate man's present accomplishments and critically evaluate man's future. Like a world traveler with a thirteen year itinerary he will move from knowledge to knowledge, cognitively enriching his awareness of the world around him. The boundaries and obligations of his apprenticeship are identical to those of his peers. He is a learner. The product yield of his apprenticeship is an education. By definition he is systematically led from the darkness of ignorance to the bright open fields of knowledge for the purpose of eventually contributing to the expansion of those same fields as a constructive thoughtful adult. Magellan, Columbus, Cortez, Alexander the Great, Pythagoras, Newton, the Pilgrims, Shakespeare, Einstein, Madame Curie, Audubon, Sir Walter Scott———thousands and thousands of explorers, inventors, contributors will all march before his eyes and ears to excite his imagination, stir his own explorative desires and present him a composite of what Man has learned about himself and his Universe and what has remained a mystery.

The path from naivete to sophistication is not a solo flight. The terranaut is not alone. Two parents and a teacher share the responsibility for the optimal outcome of his spatial apprenticeship. Many other guides may also be enlisted along the route. However each guide may express his or her influence along the way the net objective is to achieve an optimal progression toward a sophisticated maturity. The community school system is a major terrain for the aspiring terranaut. In historical perspective the child as an academic learner entitled to an education as a birthright within a free society is a new entity. In terms of "mankind time" the community elementary school is in the toddler stage of development regardless of the present state of complexity. We must keep in mind that the young child did not achieve status as a "research subject in learning experiments" until 50-60 years ago. Prior to that time he simply learned or did not and very little attention was paid to how the processes of learning took place.

Our society is committed to a principle of free public education for all of its members and is further committed to a principle of literacy. Every young child is entitled to the opportunity to learn to read, write and compute along with many other activities offered by the schools. This commitment must be honored, and it is in the honoring of that commitment and conviction that we find theoretical disagreement, contradictory research, and confusion of thought and practice. We are still in our novitiate as a teaching society and there are yet many things to be learned about learning.

The space world of the modern community school system is composed of three basic types of children. The first type enters school at the appropriate age and systematically achieves expanded mastery of school subjects year after year. As the curriculum has been plotted and becomes available to them, they grasp what is offered, integrate the new comfortably into the composite of their previous learnings, explore new cognitive horizons and progress from grade to grade, filling their mental containers with the proper amounts of knowledge year after year. They are sometimes anxious and sometimes frightened. They learn to read in the prescribed amount of time and steadily improve and expand their reading through the grades. They grasp the concepts of quantity and progressively become more competent "arithmetickers". They spell and write according to expectancy. This is the **integrating learner group** which seems to ideally represent the model on which the curriculum was based. This is the group that literally learns "as the textbook said they would". Their periodic achievement tests reflect the steady expansion of their academic knowledge. Perhaps it would be better to refer to this group as the CURRICULUM MODEL group. The percentage of this type of child varies in every classroom, building and system in the nation. Most authorities in education seem to agree that this group is in the majority in every school system. As long as this group remains in the majority the curriculum of the school system can be regarded as appropriate to society's demand that the school serve as the institution to prepare its children for adult competency.

The second population of children may be designated as the Special Education group. For a variety of reasons, they are unable to survive on a day-by-day basis in the mainstream of education and require a special curriculum to meet their needs. The deaf, blind, physically handicapped, mentally retarded, aphasic, emotionally disturbed and culturally disadvantaged compose this category.

The firmament of Special Education is filled with many constellations. Despite the labels and the diagnostic scramble, the fundamental truth on which school provisions for this population are based is one of failure. A school decision is made, at times upon entry or later after the child has been given the opportunity to achieve, to the effect that the child is not benefiting from the curriculum of the mainstream and special provisions are necessary. This it not to condemn the child as a failure in a general sense, but rather to indicate that the unique needs of this child have demanded some other form of curricula than the majority form.

The complexity of the human organism in its vulnerability to disease, injury, neglect, deprivation, psychic trauma and metabolic error has consistently been the cause of educational dilemnas. Children have frequently appeared on the Special Education doorstep with multiple problems and the educational classifier has been forced to decide which of the child's problems should take precedence over the others for purposes of school placement.

Harnessed by the artificial construct of "homogeneous groups" as the major administrative device at his disposal, the educator has been forced to form groups with the "greatest possible homogeneity that can be obtained". This enables the class to operate under the conventional wisdom that children with similar physical, mental or sensory problems will be similar in their learning. This assumption borrowed easily as a cup of sugar from the next door neighbor of elementary education has proven to be a constant migraine headache for the Special Educator, since homogeneity for classroom learning has not been easy to attain. The typical outcome of this difficulty has been the formulation of various sub-classifications within each of the major disability groups seeking to more clearly define elements of homogeneity that would permit optimal benefit from a school experience.

This second population of Special Education children is a variable percentage according to most authorities because each community school system is free to establish as many or as few special units as it may deem necessary. Throughout the nation, the complex of special units in a school system is variable from town to town and state to state. The per cent size of this second child group has been estimated from 3-20%. In consideration of the improvement in diagnostic sensitivity leading to more discrete identifications, we are inclined to accept the 20% figure as operational for Special Education.

For the sake of argument we shall arbitrarily at this moment assign a 50% figure to the population we have called the CURRICULUM MODEL group. This leaves a figure of 30% to be accounted for in the third child population. Perhaps the most apt designation for this population is that of the REMEDIAL group.

In general practice this group of children has virtually become a "limbo" group floating in mid-space between the mainstream of education and the specialized units.

2. SKILLS

This group indicates an adequate intelligence when measured by currently available instruments, demonstrates no gross sensory impairment, appears to be culturally advantaged, and while perhaps exhibiting some signs of emotional problems is not seriously disturbed. They cannot truly be classified in any of the existing Special Education categories, and yet they do not learn at the pace and with the same efficiency as the "mainstream" demands. This "limbo" group is progressively achieving identification as the Learning Disabilities population.

The community educator is painfully aware of that gnawing 30% which seems to be an inevitability. Each September eager tens of thousands of children embark upon the first grade journey towards reading competency and each following September there is little doubt that the previous nine months of school experience will have produced a **high, middle** and **low** reading group. By the time the middle and low group have struggled through another year, the referral forms for Remedial Reading service begin.

The same phenomenon of grouping may occur in arithmetic, spelling, writing, and so on. The CURRICULUM MODEL group proceeding according to schedule begins to draw further and further away from the stumbling, hesitant, confused remedial group. The Remedial group loses the cadence and is out of step in the march. Their only hope lies in a form of emergency educational first-aid to bolster their reading, arithmetic or whatever position of the academic anatomy may be wounded and returning them to the frontlines with the Model group. This first-aid corps is composed of the classroom teacher providing extra help or special assignments, the Remedial tutor removing the child from class several periods per week, the Speech Correctionist, or any others the school may add to the roster. The general thinking here is that the child is only a minor casualty and can eventually be restored to full battle status. Sometimes the first-aid is highly successful and such restoration is achieved, but many times the remedial plasma still leaves the child with an academic limp on which he hobbles for the remainder of his academic life.

These are the three child populations served by the school from age 5-18 as a general rule. There is yet a fourth population whose constellation of problems is sufficiently severe to deny them admission to a classroom program. There remains a small percentage of children who are so severely damaged physically, mentally or emotionally that they are unschoolable.

Perhaps the percentage split of 50-50 between those who achieve curricular competency and the two problem groups in the Special and Remedial categories appears to be an overstatement of the case. The figures are illustrative and intended to establish a perspective and should not be considered to have been derived from statistics. Neither should they be considered as a fictitious exaggeration. The true statistic will probably always be open to debate and question, but all community educators will attest to a growing percentage of children in each of the two problem groups. Educators will also admit that the services in any school system are rarely astride the needs.

We have almost reached a point where half the effort of a community school system is devoted to the CURRICULUM MODEL child, and the other half is devoted to the Special child in one category or another.

In the battle for educational survival the casualty rate is impressive. Every child born today will five years hence be counted in one of those three school groups. He has five years from his first cry to his kindergarten entry to make all necessary preparations to ensure his assignment to the CURRICULUM MODEL group.

Another type of educational problem which has received little attention in the literature may be termed the "diminishing achiever". Educators throughout the nation are acquainted with the problem of the child who is judged to be an adequate achiever for the first three grades of school and begins to demonstrate learning problems in his fourth grade year. The child who has been doing well until fifth grade and then begins to encounter serious difficulty is a known figure. The shift to junior high school regimen usually produces a number of learning problems among students who have previously performed at adequate levels. Senior high school also produces another percentage who become failing students after a prior record of adequacy. This phenomenon is also noted at the college level. Most colleges and universities are highly selective in their admission policies taking in only those students who have already demonstrated academic adequacy in their secondary years. The reasons for college failure may be numerous, such as immaturity, social excess, psychological problems, etc. Some segment of the college dropout percentage, however, is traceable to inadequate study habits, poor reading ability, inability to sustain a high quality effort and other percepto-cognitive difficulties. Each school year at any age is marked by a certain percentage of failures among students who, according to usual criteria, are not expected to encounter difficulty.

This entire group, from kindergarten through college, who encounter difficulties without manifesting gross signs of disorder, are also progressively acquiring a designation as learners with "special learning disabilities".

The period from kindergarten through high school must be filled with activities. Each activity must in some manner contribute to achievement of society's goals for its learners. The systematic sequence of activities leading to that goal is a **curriculum**. The typical curriculum of the community school system is based upon the premise that certain proficiencies in skills and knowledges have already been established by the time a child enrolls in kindergarten, and therefore the program of activity can be organized to **advance** a child. Not only is the curriculum designed to move forward from an "expected level of proficiency" but from a different perspective it is also defined well in advance of the present child's entry. Curriculum designers must be "in tune with the times". As each social, technological, scientific, economic and industrial advance takes place in an accelerated world, it must be incorporated into the school program. Each theorem, fact, piece of equipment or belief which has become obsolete must be deleted and appropriately replaced. A curriculum must be dynamic—in a constant state of remodeling—a current reflection of the changing times. This mandate for a dynamic curriculum places a heavy burden upon curriculum designers. If the goal of a curriculum is to ensure a progression of achievements leading to a competency for an unknown future, then the rapidity with which the world of man and his Universe is changing must indeed require a "crystal ball". What kind of world will there be and what kind of a citizen will the kindergartner of today face and be some twenty years hence? However the historians may eventually characterize this era, there is little current doubt that the curriculum of today must reflect a Space Age. Despite the magnificence of atomic energy and the hydrogen bomb, it is the penetration of the frontiers of space that will receive historical priority. The curriculum, therefore, must not only reflect the Space Age in bringing knowledge of space explorations into the classroom, but it is the contention of this book that the basic set of concepts which have led scientists to achieve orbital flight must become the core set of principles to be applied in the true understanding of the dynamic human learner.

The casualty rate in elementary, secondary and collegiate levels, as well as the casualty rate in Special Education, clearly demand some alternative strategies. The strategies thus far have been tagential and proliferated and lacking in cohesive force. Some form of strategy unification seems imperative to optimize the educational survival of all future terranauts.

THE ADULT PERIOD

We can next turn to the third terrain in the development of the earth-bound space traveler—adulthood space.
A portrait of the spatially sophisticated American leaves much to be desired. If we mount all of the evidence, we must indeed be concerned with the fact that the promise of the Basic Design somehow becomes distorted with the passage of years.

What forces are at work from infancy onward to yield the staggering statistic from authorities in posture stating that 75-85% of the adolescent population of this nation has a significant postural deviation (Lowman and Young, 1960). Apparently, 15% of the total population walk and move with the grace and ease intended by anatomical design. In twelve short years some group of factors influence a healthy organized infant who achieves erect locomotive balance to distort that balance into a postural deviation.

A President's Commission on Physical Fitness expressed a national concern for the lack of fitness among our youth and our adults. In typical American tradition billboards, posters and magazine spreads are now attempting to achieve a national awareness of the need for physical fitness much in the same manner as we are led to believe that one detergent makes clothes whiter than the next one. Advertising campaigns now direct the attention of the nation to the fact that children require special attention to their fitness.

Much of this concern was generated by a series of comparative studies testing the achievement on tests of minimum muscular fitness between American school children and those in Switzerland, Austria and Italy. The studies of Kraus and Hirschland (1954) in the eastern part of the United States, Phillips, et al, (1955) in Indiana, Fox and Atwood (1955) in Iowa, and Kirchner and Glines (1957) in Oregon, all revealed an inferiority among American children.

From these two notes, the American child already seems destined on two counts at least, to have a postural problem and to be physically unfit. A casual observation on a busy street where many people are walking will reveal the slouched shoulders, protruding stomachs, pronated ankles, sloping shoulders and tilted pelvises which bear witness to the postural problems.

The litany of adult perceptual motor efficiencies is lengthy. Few adults are skilled athletes. The weekend duffer and the 125 average bowler are common sights. Basic training instructors in all of the Armed Services will attest to the large number of enlistees who must be painstakingly taught to crawl, roll, walk, stand, run, jump, and balance in order to insure their own battlefield survival.

Dented fenders, confused parking placements, and high accident rates are continual evidence of modern man's inability to properly judge spatial distance.

Modern man is a sitting-being comfortable in his easy chair content to be an audience and only mildly interested in being a performer. His society invested thousands upon thousands of dollars to make him a skilled reader and this investment in adult life has paid the minimal dividends of reading the daily newspaper and countless advertisements. The love for reading for pleasure and information carefully nurtured by dedicated teachers during his elementary years dwindles to what might be called the "survival level" of reading—just enough to stay alive. An occasional magazine and perhaps an occasional book keep alive the reading pattern—but for the most part, reading of books is regarded as something that was associated with formal schooling—and once the demand is removed, there is little incentive to continue.

His society invested thousands upon thousands of dollars to assist him in attaining mathematical competency, but his adult life is spent in a continual apology for the fact that he was "never much good with numbers".

Personnel managers complain of poor spelling, poor handwriting, poor arithmetic, and poor reading and frequently urge educators to emphasize such training to a greater degree. The complaints are registered not regarding the retarded, the disturbed or the handicapped, but refer to high school graduates of average intelligence and often to the college graduate with above-average intelligence.

The inventive genius of man continues to supply modern man with more and more time and labor saving devices to provide more and more free time and less need to move. The achievement of man's sedentation is nearly complete. He sits through approximately 80% of his school life engaged in the near-point visual task. The vast majority of the jobs in the nation are sedentary jobs, so he probably spends 80% of his vocational life sitting. His household chores which used to offer a possibility for movement become more and more automatized so he has more time to sit and watch television. Any distance over two blocks requires him to sit and ride in his car. He sits to watch sporting events and complains if he must park his car more than a hundred yards from the gate. A future of sedentation seems assured.

The spatial confusion of many average adults who admit to a poor sense of direction suggests that the "ugly American" and the "fat American" can be joined by the "lost American".

Almost at every turn there is evidence of adult inefficiency. Postural problems, accident proneness, dietary limitations, spectatoritis, increasing numbers of traffic fatalities, job failures, uncertainties and anxieties; poor listeners and inaccurate observers abound. Incoordination is a majority finding. Errors in communication are abundantly evident. The political world is in constant turmoil. Mental illness continues to increase in incidence. Everywhere the inefficiency of man is evident, and yet the science of human understanding and the understanding of the universe has progressed more rapidly during the past twenty-five years than it has during the past several centuries.

2. SKILLS

"Obsolescence" has become a key word in the culture of today.

Three critical periods have been reviewed. The infant terranaut initiates his exploration in earth space under the guidance of parents who all seem to "wish they knew more about children", and for the most part, are eager to be more efficient. A set of constructs which could form the basis for a child-rearing curriculum in a Space Age might serve to improve parental efficiency. The school terranaut is in need of a curriculum which will reflect his own explorer identity and the Space Age in which he lives. A critical appraisal of the typical school curriculum will reveal that there is no real need to declare the curriculum obsolete. The major portions of most curricula are excellent. Rather than remodel or change the curriculum, it seems wiser to find methods to bring the learner to a higher state of learning efficiency. Changes in curricular content have a way of taking care of themselves in the due course of social change, but changes in a conceptualization of the human learner require an intensive inspection and analysis of the human terranaut as a learner. There is a need for a unified approach to curriculum at all points. Some scheme must be devised to unify curriculum concepts in both general and special education. The luxury of multiple theories and multiple curricula is uneconomical in an era of synthesis on so many other fronts. It must be possible to define a common set of practical constructs to guide the disparate elements in Special Education to a point of fusion and at the same time establish a second point of fusion with general education.

If both of these objectives, improved parental efficiency and the optimization of learning efficiency for **all** learners, could be achieved, we might produce a more efficient generation of adults. Also, if a set of constructs related to human performance efficiency could be conceived, it might serve to unify evaluative considerations at all levels of living. Perhaps a thread of efficiency must be woven into the fabric of human behavior to bind it tight at all ages.

Parental inefficiency, learner inefficiency, and adult inefficiency in a Space Age seem to provide a core of elements which might be converted into a meaningful synthesis if the negative were changed to a positive note, and the weaving of a theory were begun with the thread of EFFICIENCY. This triad of inefficiencies has become the first impulse towards a theory. The theory is called **Movigenics**.

Hyperactive Motor Disorders

Hyperactivity is a behavioral symptom which effects approximately 1 million of our children today. Youngsters who display this disorder are restless, impulsive, at times ill-mannered, uncoordinated and usually aggressive. Also, they often have difficulties learning and getting along with their peers and adults. Gardner has pointed out that

> While it may be true that physical factors account for some of the excessive motor activity, it is also true that a child may learn some of these behaviors through inadvertent reinforcement of others.

This statement supports the possibility that hyperactivity may be a social-emotional problem along with being a motor disorder.

The causes of hyperactivity appear to be varied depending on one's point of view. In many cases, this disturbance tends to be associated with some lag in social or physical maturation. Therefore, this disorder can be seen as a developmental problem rather than a brain injury. However, others have offered biological and environmental causes which could assume some neuro-logical impairment. One feature of hyperactivity does appear consistent. That is, this disturbance usually becomes less noticeable with age. Some remnants of earlier behavior such as attention and concentration difficulties may still be present, however.

Treatments for the control of hyperactivity also are many. At times, the use of drug therapy is considered. Stimulant medications such as Ritalin and Dexadrine are often prescribed. Why or how these stimulants have a paradoxical depressive effect is still unexplained.

Other medical interventions have also made their way into current literature and use. Benjamin Feingold's suggested diet which eliminates food additives is very popular with some people at this time. Cott's orthomolecular approach which prescribes massive doses of specific vitamins appears promising, also.

The major problem with the treatment of hyperactivity is that there is no definitive intervention that can be looked upon as the "total cure." More research in all of these areas must be done. Also, whatever the cause or the symptom, if the hyperactive child appears to be developing any psychological difficulties, mental health therapy should be considered.

ENVIRONMENTAL STIMULATION MODEL

SYDNEY S. ZENTALL

SYDNEY S. ZENTALL *is Assistant Professor, Department of Special Education and Rehabilitation, Eastern Kentucky University, Richmond.*

Abstract: Educational management of the hyperactive child is primarily directed toward reduction of environmental stimulation. Although social consensus is high regarding the use of this management technique, empirical support is lacking. An alternative theory is presented that is based on the homeostatic assumption that the hyperactive child is actually understimulated and hyperactive behaviors function to increase the external stimulation to approach a more optimal level. Empirical support for this homeostatic model is presented, and classroom treatment techniques derived from the theory and based on research are discussed. Suggested treatment is designed to optimize stimulation and thus reduce hyperactive children's needs to produce their own stimulation through activity.

EDUCATIONAL treatment of the hyperactive child has received little systematic attention. Suggested treatment has come mainly either from the medical practitioner based upon personal clinical experience (Wunderlich, 1969) or from educators based on classroom experience (Blanco, 1972; Farrald and Schamber, 1973).

During the 1960's, however, Cruickshank and his colleagues (Cruickshank, Bentzen, Ratzeburg, & Tannhauser, 1961; Cruickshank, Junkala, & Paul, 1968) published a treatment program for hyperactive children based upon the theoretical work of Strauss (Strauss & Lehtinen, 1947; Strauss & Kephart, 1955) and a 1 year field study (Cruickshank et al., 1961). The purpose of the field study was to test the theory that hyperactivity is precipitated by an excess of environmental stimulation. The study found performance gains over time for the treatment group; however, these gains were no greater than those for the traditional control group. In spite of these inconclusive results and other lack of support, including contrary findings (Zentall, 1975), the theory and derived treatment program have been widely accepted by educators (Kirk, 1972, pp. 48-50; Wasserman, Asch, & Snyder, 1972; Alabiso, 1972; Haring, 1974, p. 245).

Alternative Model

This article provides an alternative theoretical model for hyperactivity—a theory that is based on the proposition that environmental stimulation acts to decrease rather than increase hyperactivity. Research relevant to these theories is reviewed briefly and treatment implications are presented.

To facilitate comparison of the two theories, it is helpful to imagine a schematic representation of normal children with stimulus input (environmental stimulation) coming into them and response output (activity) leaving them. Within them is a stimulus filter, a hypothetical construct that provides a mech-

"Environmental Stimulation Model", Sydney S. Zentall, *Exceptional Children* Vol. 43, No. 8, May 1977, © 1977, The Council for Exceptional Children.

anism for screening incoming stimulation. Most children encounter a vast array of stimulation from which they learn to select the most relevant aspects. Typically, they function as follows: Normal environmental stimulation proceeds through the normal filter, producing sufficient stimulation for them; they are naturally active.

The overstimulation model proposed by Strauss and Lehtinen (1947) and popularized by Cruickshank and others (1961) views the hyperactive child as being overstimulated due to an inadequate stimulus filter, resulting in poor selectivity in processing stimuli or the inability to ignore irrelevant stimuli (Strauss & Lehtinen, 1947). The hyperactive child is unable to adequately filter normal incoming stimulation, creating a flood of stimulation that overwhelms the child. According to this theory, the flood of stimulation results directly in a flood of response output.

According to the model, activity serves no function for the child but merely acts as an undirected response to overstimulation. When a hyperactive child "whose reactibility is beyond his own control is placed in a situation of constant and widespread stimulation, he can only meet the situation with persistent undirected response" (Strauss & Lehtinen, 1947, p. 129).

Treatment implications of the overstimulation model are straightforward and involve maximal reduction of environmental stimulation. The total environment should be neutralized, "and every possible unessential stimulus in the classroom must be reduced in its visual, auditory or tactual impressiveness" (Cruickshank et al., 1961, p. 131).

However, observations of hyperactive children (Zuk, 1963), including those by proponents of Strauss' theory (Strauss & Lehtinen, 1947; Cruickshank, Junkala, & Paul, 1968), have often included descriptions of hyperactive children in low stimulation environments which do not support Strauss' overstimulation theory. In high stimulation environments (e.g., strange, novel situations; games; movies; on the playground), hyperactive children cannot be differentiated from normal children (Kaspar, Millichap, Backus, & Schulman, 1971; Stewart, 1970; Zentall, 1975).

Such findings and observations suggest the hypothesis that environmental stimulation does not cause hyperactivity but in fact may reduce it. If so, what kind of mechanism might normalize hyperactive children by increasing environmental stimulation? Initially, it must be assumed that there is a basic need or drive for stimulation (Leuba, 1955, p. 29; Berlyne, 1960) and that for each child there is some level of stimulation that is optimal in a given environment. Also, like other drives, there is a homeostatic control mechanism that attempts to increase stimulus input when stimulation falls below the optimal level. Just as hungry organisms will search for food, so an understimulated organism will search for stimulation. Stimulus input can be increased by increasing locomotor activity or verbalizations or by changing the orientation of the receptors (e.g., movement of the head or eyes) to allow more and varied stimulation to reach the eyes and ears, which are behaviors all typical of the hyperactive syndrome.

If, in fact, the hyperactive child suffers from understimulation rather than overstimulation, it may be that the hyperactive child overfilters stimulus input such that normal stimulation is effectively blocked off from the child thereby reducing incoming stimulation to unacceptable levels. According to such an optimal stimulation model, hyperactive behavior is not undirected but serves to provide the hyperactive child with needed stimulus input.

Empirical Support

The majority of studies that have manipulated visual and auditory stimulation have used hyperactive retarded children and have found decreases in activity with increases in sensory stimulation (Gardner, Cromwell, & Foshee, 1959; Cleland, 1962; Tizard, 1968; Forehand & Baumeister, 1970; Reardon & Bell, 1970) except when stimulation was noxious or nonmeaningful (e.g., white noise or speeded language) in which case the increased sensory stimulation appeared to have little effect on activity (Spradlin, Cromwell, & Foshee, 1959; Levitt & Kaufman, 1965; Steinschneider, Lipton, & Richmond, 1966).

Studies that used normal IQ subjects have also found decreased activity with increased visual and auditory environmental stimulation (Scott, 1970; Zentall & Zentall, 1976). Zentall and Zentall (1976), using a counterbalanced, repeated measures design, compared activity and performance of hyperactive children under conditions of high and low environmental stimulation. The hyperactive children were significantly less active and performed better (although not significantly better) in the high stimulation environment than in the low stimulation environment.

Evidence from other studies that have measured performance suggests (contrary to predictions from the overstimulation theory) that increased distal environmental stimulation does not disrupt visual task performance with (a) retarded, nonhyperactive populations (Cruse, 1961; Ellis, Hawkins, Pryer, & Jones, 1973; see Gorton, 1972, for an exception); (b) hyperactive, retarded populations (Cromwell & Foshee, 1960; Burnette, 1962); (c) hyperactive normal IQ populations (Rost & Charles, 1967; Shores & Haubrich, 1969; Scott, 1970; Zentall & Zentall, 1976); or (d) distractible normal IQ populations (Somervill, Warnberg, & Bost, 1973). After reviewing several of the above studies, Dunn (1973) also concluded, "This sample of literature casts considerable doubt on the necessity of the Strauss-Lehtinen classroom environment for hyperactive and brain-injured children" (p. 558).

While there is some evidence that children look at their visual tasks more when there is nothing else to look at (i.e., when isolated in low stimulation cubicles), there is no corresponding performance gains (Shores & Haubrich, 1969). In fact, studies that have reported using combined visual and auditory distal stimulation with normal IQ populations (Scott, 1970; Zentall & Zentall, 1976) have found tendencies for hyperactive individuals to perform better on visual tasks (although in neither case were the effects significant).

Similarly, task performance is not adversely affected by peripheral distracting stimulation (i.e., on the boundaries of the task and/or within the child's peripheral vision); in fact, under certain conditions minimally brain dysfunctioned children do better with increased peripheral stimulation (Browning, 1967; Carter & Diaz, 1971).

These findings raise several questions. If, in fact, children spend less time looking at their tasks in high stimulation environments, why is it that their performance does not suffer. Time spent looking at a task appears to be a necessary but certainly not a sufficient aspect of good task performance. That is, an increase in the time spent looking at a task may not mean increased attention (i.e., meaningful attention) to the task, but may involve what is sometimes called dead-man's behavior (the child is looking at his task but not thinking about it).

While greater visual attention to tasks results in no greater performance gain, why should an increase in performance result with certain combinations of high stimulation (assuming again that the child may look away from his task more)? Browning (1967) concluded that improved performance under conditions of high peripheral stimulation was produced by attention to the stimulus enriched environment that served to maintain alertness in minimally brain dysfunctioned children, and thereby increased their readiness to respond to the task. Alternatively, in spite of repeated breaks in task to take in the high stimulation environment, children are able to attend better to the task during the time they spend on the task. That is, they are able to use the time spent on the task more efficiently. They may be able to make up for lost time and equal or even surpass performance that would have occurred under conditions of low stimulation.

Overall, there is little empirical support for Strauss' theory, a fact that even Cruickshank admits: "The emphasis on theoretical consistency within the professions is stressed here because of the absence of any substantial amount of experimental data" (Cruickshank et al., 1967, p. 15).

Sensory Deprivation

Analogous to the assumed state of sensory deprivation in hyperactive individuals is the known state of sensory deprivation in normal adults (e.g., stimulus input from the environment is reduced by placing the subject in an empty padded room). Subjects' reactions to sensory deprivation where they are free to move about include increased activity and restlessness (Heron, Doane, & Scott, 1956; Sato & Tada, 1970; Altman, 1971; Sales, 1971), which are behaviors that could be interpreted as attempts to increase stimulus input.

Experiments that restrict the subject's ability to move produce a far greater reduction in functioning. Participants often display concentration problems, disorganization of thought (Scott, Bexton, Heron, & Doane, 1954; Freedman & Greenblatt, 1960), and changes in electroencephalogram that persist even beyond the experiment (Heron et al., 1956).

These behavioral reactions to stimulus deprivation are similar to behavioral descriptions of hyperactive children. Cromwell, Baumeister, and Hawkins (1963, p. 64) suggest that while hyperactive children appear to have intact sensory apparatus, they behave as though they were sensory deprived. The poor visual motor test performance seen in sensory deprived normals (Laufer, Denhoff, & Solomons, 1957; Clements & Peters, 1962) also parallels the poor visual-motor test performance of hyperactive children (Douglas, 1972). Furthermore, Zubek (1963) found that in normal adults, periods of increased activity could reduce the impaired performance produced by sensory deprivation. Activity, therefore, appears to function similarly for hyperactives and sensory deprived normals.

Effects of Amphetamine Drugs

One of the apparent paradoxes associated with hyperactive children is that stimulant drugs such as Ritalin and amphetamines behaviorally calm the hyperactive children instead of making them more active. The traditional explanation for the drug's calming effect is that the drugs operate on different mechanisms in hyperactive children than they do in normal children. In normal children, stimulant drugs activate excitatory systems leading to an increase in arousal and activity; in hyperactive children the same drugs activate inhibitory systems leading to a decrease in arousal and activity (Ritvo, 1975; Wender, 1971).

The alternative and simpler explanation for the calming effects of stimulant drugs on hyperactive children is that: (a) the drugs have a consistent arousal producing function in all children, and (b) hyperactive children are underaroused, and the drugs maintain an adequate level of arousal reducing their need to provide themselves with additional stimulation through hyperactive behavior. This underarousal view of hyperactivity is supported by various physiological measures of arousal, including lower skin conductance levels, higher mean electroencephalogram amplitudes, and larger evoked cortical response amplitudes (Satterfield, Cantwell, & Satterfield, 1974). Such data are consistent with the position that hyperactive children are inefficient in their use of naturally occurring environmental stimulation due to excessive stimulus filtering. According to such a filter theory, stimulant drugs reduce the amount of filtering and allow for more efficient use of existing stimulus input.

While the effectiveness of amphetamine drug therapy can be explained in terms of the understimulation theory, it is a medical not an educational treatment. Furthermore, even as a medical treatment it involves unwanted short

term and long term side effects (Freedman, 1966; Cohen & Douglas, 1972). For these reasons, educators continue to look for treatments that involve environmental rather than medical manipulations.

To summarize, there are three ways in which hyperactive children can approach an optimal level of stimulation in low stimulation environments (e.g., waiting):

1. Stimulant drugs can make the processing of existing stimulation more efficient, thus eliminating the need to produce stimulation through physical movement. Because the children no longer need to create their own stimulation, the drug appears to have a behavioral calming effect; but, it may also have short term or long term side effects.

2. The children's own activity can increase stimulation. However, self produced activity tends to be disruptive in most school environments.

3. Environmental stimulation can be increased directly, providing perhaps the best means of approaching optimal levels of stimulation without introducing unwanted behavioral or medical side effects.

The remainder of this article will describe ways of increasing environmental stimulation for the hyperactive child in a school setting with the aim of decreasing hyperactive behavior and increasing academic performance.

Treatment through Environmental Control

If an understimulation model of hyperactivity is accepted, in what ways can teachers arrange the classroom environment to minimize hyperactive behavior and maximize performance?

General Setting

Instead of maintaining a small grey stimulus impoverished classroom with carrels facing blank walls, it is proposed that large rooms be subdivided into center of interest areas such as social, exploratory, and mastery centers as proposed by Hewett (1968). Following are suggestions for the makeup of these areas:

- *Color and patterns.* Center of interest areas should be decorated with bright posters and pictures or bulletin boards that should be changed frequently because high levels of distal visual stimulation appear to be an important variable in reducing activity (Gardner et al., 1959; Tizard, 1968; Forehand & Baumeister, 1970; Zentall & Zentall, 1976).

• *Movement.* Some form of movement should exist in the classroom such as pets (mice or guinea pigs in habit trails, fish in tanks), mobiles, or other children moving from task to task. While the hyperactive child may attend to this movement from time to time, the net effect may be a reduction in hyperactive behavior and either no effect on performance or a slight gain. Desks facing windows may be an excellent way of providing movement and varied stimulation.

• *Duration.* Since sensory input undergoes adaptation, a given level of stimulation may be less effective over time. For this reason, tasks should be short. Activity has been shown to increase with increased exposure to a repetitive task (e.g., listening to tones, vigilance, continuous performance task) regardless of whether performance is high, as with a task in which continuous reinforcement is used (Cohen, 1970; Cohen & Douglas, 1972), or low (Douglas, 1974). Furthermore, an increase in activity is most often accompanied by a corresponding deterioration in performance (Douglas, 1974; Zentall, Zentall, & Booth, 1976).

• *Novelty.* The length of exposure to a task that a hyperactive child can tolerate appears to depend upon the amount of prior familiarization or exposure to that task. The longer a child is exposed to a task, the more the task will tend to lose its novelty and the more hyperactive behavior is likely to occur (Tizard, 1968; Reardon & Bell, 1970). The increase in activity that occurs over time during task performance (especially during tasks that are repetitive) has been interpreted by Reardon and Bell (1970) and Cohen and Douglas (1971) as an attempt to increase the novelty of stimulus input. Frequent changes in tasks may be sufficient to maintain novelty over long periods.

Although increases in distal and peripheral stimulation do not disrupt and may actually improve task performance for the hyperactive or minimally brain dysfunctioned child (Browning, 1967; Scott, 1970; Carter & Diaz, 1971; Zentall & Zentall, 1976), recent unpublished research suggests that if the increased stimulation is incorporated into the task (e.g., by coloring task figures), performance by the hyperactive children may be disrupted more than performance of normal children (Zentall, Zentall, & Barack, 1976) or may be disrupted for a longer time than for normal children (Zentall, Zentall, & Booth, 1976). Therefore, the locus of added stimulation may be important in determining its effect on task performance. The addition of stimulation directly to the task figures may increase attention to the task, but it may also embed the task within the added stimulation, thus making it difficult to separate the task from the added stimulation. These findings are counter to Hallahan and Kauffman's (1976, pp. 160 & 162) endorsement of Cruickshank and others' (1961) suggestions to use vivid color stimulation in instructional materials.

Practically, the results suggest that added stimulation should be placed outside the physical boundaries of the task items, either spatially (e.g., in the distal or peripheral environment) or temporally (e.g., prior to performance of the task).

• *Task difficulty.* Tasks that insure success seem to be essential to maintained attention in children. Meichenbaum and Goodman (1969) have demonstrated that the performance of impulsive children deteriorated more rapidly than normal's as task difficulty increased. Normals also persist longer at difficult intellectual tasks (Kagan, Pearson, & Welch, 1966) and at difficult fine motor tasks (Pope, 1970). These differences in persistence were noted in spite of equivalent initial abilities in the normal and hyperactive groups.

Jacobs (1972) reported no differences between hyperactive and normal children on simple, reaction time and motor tasks in which a simple response (e.g., release a key) was made to the onset of a light signal. Differences between the groups emerged, however, in more difficult decision making tasks (e.g., go/no-go tasks).

• *Large group tasks.* One of the most *difficult* tasks for hyperactive children (i.e., a task that differentiates normal from hyperactive children) involves waiting (Pope, 1970). It may be for this reason that hyperactive children are perceived by teachers as difficult to control in teacher directed group tasks that, for example, involve one child who is performing (e.g., reading) while the others wait their turn. Similarly, on group achievement tests that typically involve teacher paced directions dependent upon prespecified time periods or the performance of the slowest child, hyperactive children show performance deficits (Douglas, 1974). On the other hand, in tasks that involve a one to one relationship, such as tutoring or individual testing, hyperactive children cannot be distinguished from normals (Douglas, 1974). Cruickshank and his colleagues (1961, pp. 162-163) have argued that group tasks are more difficult for hyperactive children because they involve high levels of stimulation, with which the hyperactive child cannot cope. But the fact that group tasks typically require periods of waiting patiently for the teacher's attention and a lower teacher to child ratio (as source of stimulation) suggests that such tasks result in poorer performance and hyperactivity because they provide low rather than high stimulation.

● *Self paced tasks.* Douglas (1974) has demonstrated that hyperactive children are more proficient on tasks in which they can regulate the rate at which they progress, than on tasks that are experimenter paced. The difference in performance can be attributed to the elimination of waiting and the opportunity for control of stimulus input provided by self paced tasks.

● *Active tasks.* Tasks that involve movement and active participation appear to be particularly appropriate for hyperactive children. For instance, tasks that require structured movements in their performance (e.g., pegboard tasks) have been reported to be more successful than tasks that involve waiting (Pope, 1970).

Adding activity to task performance, however, can create other problems. Care should be taken that the activity does not interfere with task performance by encouraging the child to focus more on the activity produced than on the task. To reduce the likelihood of activity produced interference, especially during information acquisition, activity should either not be included during early stages of task learning (Zentall, Zentall, & Booth, 1976) or be restricted to the period following task completion.

Activities following tasks may be particularly important to hyperactive children because directed movement has been demonstrated to reduce performance impairments produced by sensory deprivation (Zubek, 1963). Some examples are: (a) having the children move to different parts of the classroom (i.e., centers) whenever a change in task occurs (initially as often as every 10 to 15 minutes, depending upon the child), (b) having them deliver messages to the main office or another class after a specified task has been completed, (c) giving them two seats if they have difficulty staying in one, (d) teaching them isometric exercises that they could perform when it becomes difficult to sit still, and (e) giving them short periods of imposed exercises.

Reinforcement versus Environmental Stimulation

● *Isolation.* If isolation from the classroom group to a cubicle or a time out room is effective in reducing hyperactive behavior, it probably is not for the reasons typically given. That is, the condition of sensory deprivation (e.g., cubicle) may actually increase hyperactive behavior while the child is isolated, but it may result in improved behavior when the child is permitted to return to the classroom. The following two reasons account for the improved behavior: (a) Isolation serves as punishment for the hyperactive behavior that preceded it, and (b) return to the classroom provides novel stimulation especially when compared to the sensory deprivation produced by isolation.

● *Reinforcement.* In contrast to the use of punishment or the threat of punishment is the more frequently used and experimentally tested use of positive reinforcement to increase appropriate nonhyperactive behaviors (e.g., sitting). While reinforcement has been demonstrated to increase appropriate behaviors (Allen, Henke, Harris, Baer, & Reynolds, 1969; Dubros & Daniels, 1966; Pihl, 1967), the effect of this treatment may not persist over time under normal classroom conditions (Quay, Sprague, Werry, & McQueen, 1966; Freibergs & Douglas, 1969). The short term effect has been attributed to the dependency of the hyperactive child on high rates of reinforcement. Rapid extinction of appropriate responses often occurs when reinforcement is partially withdrawn (Douglas, 1974). It may be that reinforcers also serve as needed sources of stimulation such that when they are withdrawn the need for stimulus input is filled by hyperactive behavior.

To make reinforcement therapy more effective, other sources of stimulation should be found to replace those lost when reinforcers are faded out. Alternatively, reinforcers can be internalized by teaching hyperactive children techniques of self control through self verbalizations (Santostefano & Stayton, 1967;

Palkes, Stewart, & Kahana, 1968; Meichenbaum & Goodman, 1971). These techniques involve teaching them to talk to themselves using such strategies as planning ahead, stopping to think, being careful, correcting errors calmly, and rewarding oneself for using the appropriate strategy (Meichenbaum & Goodman, 1971).

Conclusions

Derived from the theory that hyperactivity is related to understimulation are treatments that differ radically from the most widely practiced nonmedical treatment of hyperactivity. Results of a large number of studies support an understimulation model. Furthermore, the results of research that has reported stimulant drugs and selective reinforcement of nonhyperactive behavior effective in controlling hyperactivity are consistent with the understimulation model since, in both cases, they can function to increase effective stimulation for the child.

It is quite possible that the modality and nature of increased stimulation that will result in reduced hyperactivity will differ from child to child. Further research will indicate whether this is so, and may provide a better understanding of not only the physiological mechanism underlying hyperactivity but also the general sensory filtering mechanism.

It may be that a simple understimulation model is insufficient to account for the behavior of all children that have been labeled hyperactive, because they are not a homogeneous population. Wider educational use of high stimulation environments will also help to determine which aspects of increased stimulation are most effective and the extent to which increased environmental stimulation can generally improve behavior and performance of not only hyperactive children but all children suffering from understimulation (i.e., boredom) as well.

References

Alabiso, F. Inhibitory functions of attention in reducing hyperactive behavior. *American Journal of Mental Deficiency*, 1972, 77, 259-282.

Allen, E., Henke, L. B., Harris, F., Baer, D. M., & Reynolds, J. J. Control of hyperactivity by social reinforcement of attending behavior. In R. C. Anderson, G. W. Faust, M. C. Roderick, D. J. Cunningham, & T. Andre (Eds.), *Current research on instruction*. Englewood Cliffs NJ: Prentice-Hall, 1969.

Altman, R. The influence of brief social deprivation on activity of mentally retarded children. *Training School Bulletin*, 1971, 68, 165-169.

Berlyne, E. *Conflict, arousal and curiosity.* New York: McGraw-Hill, 1960.

Blanco, R. F. *Prescriptions for children with learning and adjustment problems.* Springfield IL. Charles C Thomas, 1972.

Browning, R. M. Hypo-responsiveness as a behavioral correlate of brain-damage in children. *Psychological Reports*, 1967, 20, 251-259.

Burnette, E. Influences of classroom environment on work learning of retarded with high and low activity levels. Unpublished doctoral dissertation, Peabody College, 1962.

Carter, J. L., & Diaz, A. Effects of visual and auditory background on reading test performance. *Exceptional Children*, 1971, 38, 43-50.

Cleland, C. C. Severe retardation—Program suggestions. *Training School Bulletin*, 1962, 59, 31-37.

Clements, S. D., & Peters, J. E. Minimal brain dysfunction in the school-age child. *Archives of General Psychiatry*, 1962, 6, 185-197.

Cohen, N. J. Psychophysiological concomitants of attention in hyperactive children. Unpublished doctoral dissertation, McGill University, 1970.

Cohen, N. J., & Douglas, V. I. Characteristics of the orienting response in hyperactive and normal children. *Psychophysiology*, 1972, 9, 238-245.

Cohen, N.J., & Douglas, V. I. Effects of reward on attention in hyperactive children. Unpublished manuscript, McGill University, 1971. (Available from V. I. Douglas, McGill University, Montreal, Canada.)

Cromwell, R. L., Baumeister, A., & Hawkins, W. F. Research in activity level. In N. R. Ellis (Ed.), *Handbook of mental deficiency*. New York: McGraw-Hill, 1963.

Cromwell, R. L., & Foshee, J. G. Studies in activity level: IV. Effects of visual stimulation during task performance in mental defectives. *American Journal of Mental Deficiency*, 1960, 65, 248-251.

Cruickshank, W. M., Bentzen, F. A., Ratzeburg, F. H., & Tannhauser, M. T. *A teaching method for brain-injured and hyperactive children: A demonstration pilot study.* Syracuse NY: Syracuse University Press, 1961.

Cruickshank, W. M., Junkala, J. B., & Paul, J. L. *The preparation of teachers of the brain-injured and hyperactive children.* Syracuse NY: Syracuse University Press, 1968.

Cruse, D. B. Effects of distraction upon the performance of brain-injured and familial retarded children. *American Journal of Mental Deficiency*, 1961, 66, 86-92.

Douglas, V. I. Stop, look and listen: The problem of sustained attention and impulse control. *Canadian Journal of Behavioral Science*, 1972, 4, 259-282.

Douglas, V. I. Sustained attention and impulse control: Implications for the handicapped child. In J. A. Swets & L. L. Elliott (Eds.), *Psychology and the handicapped child*. Washington DC: US Government Printing Office, 1974.

Dubros, S. G., & Daniels, G. J. An experimental approach to the reduction of over-active behavior. *Behavior Research and Therapy*, 1966, *4*, 251-258.

Dunn, L. M. (Ed.). *Exceptional children in the schools.* New York: Holt, Rinehart & Winston, 1973.

Ellis, N. R., Hawkins, W. F., Pryer, M., & Jones, R. W. Distraction effects in oddity learning by normal and mentally defective humans. *American Journal of Mental Deficiency*, 1963, *67*, 576-583.

Farrald, R. R., & Schamber, R. G. *A diagnostic and prescriptive technique: Handbook 1: A mainstream approach to identification, assessment and amelioration of learning disabilities.* Sioux Falls SD: Adapt Press, Inc., 1973.

Forehand, R., & Baumeister, A. A. Effects of variations in auditory and visual stimulation on activity levels of severe mental retardates. *American Journal of Mental Deficiency*, 1970, *74*, 470-474.

Freedman, S. J., & Greenblatt, M. Studies in human isolation I. Perceptual findings. *Armed Forces Medical Journal*, 1960, *11*, 1330-1348.

Freedman, R. D. Drug effects on learning in children: A selective review of the past thirty years. *Journal of Special Education*, 1966, *1*, 17-44.

Freibergs, V., & Douglas, V. I. Concept learning in hyperactive and normal children. *Journal of Abnormal Psychology*, 1969, *74*, 388-395.

Gardner, W. I., Cromwell, R. L., & Foshee, J. G. Studies in activity level. II. Effects of distal visual stimulation in organics, familials, hyperactives. *American Journal of Mental Deficiency*, 1959, *63*, 1028-1033.

Gorton, C. E. The effects of various classroom environments on performance of a mental task by mentally retarded and normal children. *Education and Training of the Mentally Retarded*, 1972, *7*, 32-38.

Hallahan, D. P., & Kauffman, J. M. *Introduction to learning disabilities.* Englewood Cliffs NJ: Prentice-Hall, 1976.

Haring, N. G. *Behavior of exceptional children.* Columbus OH: Charles E. Merrill, 1974.

Heron, W., Doane, B. K., & Scott, T. H. Visual disturbances after prolonged perceptual isolation. *Canadian Journal of Psychology*, 1956, *10*, 13-18.

Hewett, F. M. *The emotionally disturbed child in the classroom.* Boston: Allyn & Bacon, 1968.

Jacobs, N. T. A comparison of hyperactive and normal boys in terms of reaction time, motor time, and decision-making time, under conditions of increasing task complexity. Unpublished doctoral dissertation, University of California, 1972.

Kagan, J., Pearson, L., & Welch, L. The modifiability of an impulsive tempo. *Journal of Educational Psychology*, 1966, *57*, 359-365.

Kaspar, J. C., Millichap, J. G., Backus, D. C., & Schulman, J. L. A study of the relationship between neurological evidence of brain damage in children and activity and distractibility. *Journal of Consulting and Clinical Psychology*, 1971, *36*, 329-337.

Kirk, S. P. *Educating Exceptional Children.* Boston: Houghton Mifflin Company, 1972.

Laufer, M. W., Denhoff, E., & Solomons, G. Hyperkinetic impulse disorder in children's behavior problems. *Psychosomatic Medicine*, 1957, *19*, 38-49.

Leuba, C. Toward some integration of learning theories: The concept of optimal stimulation. *Psychological Reports*, 1955, *1*, 27-33.

Levitt, H. & Kaufman, M. E. Sound induced drive and stereotyped behavior in mental defectives. *American Journal of Mental Deficiency*, 1965, *69*, 729-734.

Meichenbaum, D. H., & Goodman, J. The developmental control of operant motor responding by verbal operants. *Journal of Experimental Child Psychology*, 1969, *7*, 553-565.

Meichenbaum, D. H., & Goodman, J. Training impulsive children to talk to themselves: A means of developing self-control. *Journal of Abnormal Psychology*, 1971, *77*, 115-126.

Palkes, H., Stewart, M., & Kahana, B. Porteus maze performance of hyperactive boys after training in self-directed verbals commands. *Child Development*, 1968, *39*, 817-826.

Pihl, R. O. Conditioning procedures with hyperactive children. *Neurology*, 1967, *17*, 421-423.

Pope, L. Motor activity in brain injured children. *American Journal of Orthopsychiatry*, 1970, *40*, 783-793.

Quay, J., Sprague, R., Werry, J., & McQueen, M. Conditioning visual orientation of conduct problem children in the classroom. *Journal of Experimental Child Psychology*, 1966, *5*, 512-517.

Reardon, D. M., & Bell, G. Effects of sedative and stimulative music on activity levels of severely retarded boys. *American Journal of Mental Deficiency*, 1970, *75*, 156-159.

Ritvo, E. R. Biochemical research with hyperactive children. In D. P. Cantwell (Ed.), *The hyperactive child.* New York: John Wiley & Sons, 1975.

Rost, K. J., & Charles, D. C. Academic achievement of brain injured and hyperactive children in isolation. *Exceptional Children*, 1967, *34*, 125-126.

Sales, S. M. Need for stimulation as a factor in social behavior. *Journal of Personality and Social Psychology*, 1971, *19*, 124-134.

Santostefano, S., & Stayton, S. Training the preschool retarded child in focusing attention: A program for parents. *American Journal of Orthopsychiatry*, 1967, *37*, 732-743.

Sato, S. I., & Tada, H. Studies of sensory overload: 11. Results of psychological tests: 111. *Tohoku Psychological Folica*, 1970, *2*, 59-64.

Satterfield, H., Cantwell, D. P., & Satterfield, B. T. Pathophysiology of the hyperactive child syndrome. *Archives of General Psychiatry*, 1974, *31*, 839-844.

Scott, T. J. The use of music to reduce hyperactivity in children. *American Journal of Orthopsychiatry*, 1970, *40*, 677-680.

Scott, T. H., Bexton, W. H., Heron, W., & Doane, B. K. Cognitive effects of perceptual isolation. *Cana-*

dian *Journal of Psychology*, 1954, *13*, 200-209.

Shores, R. E., & Haubrich, P. A. Effect of cubicles in educating emotionally disturbed children. *Exceptional Children*, 1969, *36*, 21-24.

Somervill, J. W., Warnberg, L. S., & Bost, D. E. Effects of cubicles versus increased stimulation on task performance by first grade males perceived as distractible and nondistractible. *The Journal of Special Education*, 1973, *7*, 169-185.

Spradlin, J. E., Cromwell, R. L., & Foshee, J. G. Studies in activity level. 111. Effects of auditory stimulation in organics, familials, hyperactives and hypoactives. *American Journal of Mental Deficiency*, 1959, *64*, 754-757.

Steinschneider, A., Lipton, E. L., & Richmond, J. B. Auditory sensitivity in the infant: Effect of intensity of cardiac and motor responsivity. *Child Development*, 1966, *37*, 233-252.

Stewart, M. A. Hyperactive children. *Scientific American*, 1970, *222*, 94-98.

Strauss, A. A., & Kephart, N. C. *Psychopathology and education of the brain-injured child*. (Vol. II). New York: Grune & Stratton, 1955.

Strauss, A. A., & Lehtinen, L. E. *Psychopathology and education of the brain-injured child*. New York: Grune & Stratton, 1947.

Tizard, B. E. Experimental studies of over-active imbecile children. *American Journal of Mental Deficiency*, 1968, *72*, 548-553.

Wasserman, E., Asch, J., & Snyder, E. E. A neglected aspect of learning disabilities. *Journal of Learning Disabilities*, 1972, *5*, 130-135.

Wender, D. *Minimal brain dysfunction in children*. New York: Wiley Interscience, 1971.

Wunderlich, R. C. Hyperkinetic disease. *Academic Therapy*, 1969, *5*, 99-108.

Zentall, S. S. Optimal stimulation as theoretical basis of hyperactivity. *American Journal of Orthopsychiatry*, 1975, *45*, 549-563.

Zentall, S. S., & Zentall, T. R. Activity and task performance of hyperactive children as a function of environmental stimulation. *Journal of Consulting and Clinical Psychology*, 1976, *44*, 693-697.

Zentall, S. S., Zentall, T. R., & Barack, R. S. *Distraction as a function of within-task stimulation for hyperactive and normal children*. Manuscript submitted for publication, 1976. (Available from S. S. Zentall, Eastern Kentucky University, Richmond.)

Zentall, S. S., Zentall, T. R., & Booth, M. E. *Within-task stimulation: Effects on activity and spelling performance in hyperactive and normal children*. Manuscript submitted for publication, 1976. (Available from S. S. Zentall, Eastern Kentucky University, Richmond.)

Zubeck, J. P. Counteracting effects of physical exercises performed during prolonged perceptual deprivation. *Science*, 1963, *142*, 504-506.

Zuk, G. Over-attention to moving stimuli as a factor in the distractibility of retarded and brain-injured children. *Training School Bulletin*, 1963, *59*, 150-160.

HYPERKINETIC AGGRAVATION OF LEARNING DISTURBANCE

Robert Buckley

Robert Buckley, MD, 22455 Maple Court, Hayward, California, 94541, is a physician in private practice with specialty in psychosomatic medicine and psychiatry.

A rather conservative pediatric neurologist, Robert Sieben, MD, has felt compelled to write an article to warn the teaching profession that charlatans are about, offering therapy and training to the learning disordered. He feels that some of this therapy is worthless and that vitamins may even be dangerous. Yet Dr. Sieben has not followed scientific protocol in his article, since he has not discussed or defined the disorders which these children have. Perhaps he wants to avoid discussing the complicated physiology of these disorders as a result of constraints of space, or perhaps because he knows that teachers would then expect him to present some rational proposals for therapy. While he criticises the therapeutic efforts of others, he has been cautious not to propose any therapy which can be tested. Dr. Sieben has not criticized the use of stimulant drugs, and he thereby implies that he does not oppose them.

The state of hyperkinesis is one of increased motor activity, impulsiveness, distractability, and impaired motor coordination. Most hyperkinetic children have an elevated pain threshhold. As a result, they often ignore punishment and disregard danger. They have been called "fearless and foolish" (Buckley 1972). Hyperkinesis does not lead to any specific type of dyslexia or learning disorder, but it can complicate any or all of them. Should diet or medication help a hyperkinetic child, the learning disturbance will probably remain, but at a less disturbing level. C. Keith Conners, PhD, has identified seven subgroups of hyperkinesis (1973). This finding supports the proposals that several kinds of causative factors can unite to cause the nervous system to become quite irritable.

One of the factors which can cause hyperkinesis is found in the junk foods which can usually be purchased from candy stores just down the street from the school. There can be a remarkable similarity of symptoms from food allergy per se, and from sensitivity to organic chemical additives which are present in those foods. In the infant, the food which is most likely to cause colic and sleep disorders is cow's milk, followed by wheat, corn, chocolate, and citrus. These foods can cause behavior problems in older children, but the kind of disorder changes as the child matures.

The medical profession has had some controversy about the distinction between allergy and sensitivity. The allergic reactions are conceded to occur when an antigen-antibody reaction has caused the release of special chemicals from the affected cells. The food color sensitivity has an unknown mechanism for action, and so certain conservative physicians would prefer to maintain that it did not happen. It is quite difficult to understand why any cautious physician would hesitate to advise that a possible toxic chemical be withdrawn from the diet and then see if the child got better.

There is yet another problem in his comments about allergy responses. He states that the brain cannot be the "target organ" of allergic reactions because the white blood cells cannot pass the blood brain barrier. He is saying, in effect, that the presence of antibody-type chemicals in white blood cells is the sole means for causing allergic reactions. This is not correct; the topic is far more complicated.

The dubious position of Dr. Sieben is shown in his discussion of the double-blind study which Dr. Conners (of the University of Pittsburgh) published last year (1976). Dr. Sieben has selected several sentences out of context in order to imply that Conners proved that such a diet was worthless. The following paragraph is from the discussion section of the paper.

> The results of this study strongly suggest that a diet free of most natural salicylates, artificial flavors, and the artificial colors reduces the perceived hyperactivity of some children suffering from hyperkinetic impulse disorder. Teachers who observed the children over a 12-week period without knowledge of when the child started his diet and without knowledge of the fact that there were two diets which were employed, rated the children as less hyperactive while the children were on the diet recommended by [Benjamin] Feingold. The difference obtained between the ratings when the children were on the K-P Diet and when they were on the control diet would have occurred by chance only 5 in 1,000 times. Similarly, the teachers rated the children as significantly improved over the baseline period on the K-P Diet but not while on the control diet.

One major fault of this paper is that Dr. Sieben has not properly searched the medical literature for information about sensitivity to food dyes. He has read Dr. Feingold's book, *Why Your Child Is Hyperactive* (1975), but he appears to believe that Dr. Feingold created this diet from his own medical practice. In fact, food dye sensitivity was reported almost thirty years ago.

Thirty Years of Research

To my knowledge, the first paper on food dye sensitivity

was published by Steven Lockey, an allergist in Lancaster, Pennsylvania, in 1948. Every allergist is concerned with the symptomatic patient who does not get much help from desensitization shots. Dr. Lockey used a special exclusion diet for these people, and had them avoid aspirin and any foods containing salicylates. In the 1950s he proposed that the salicylate-free diet should also exclude junk food, and particularly the FD and C Yellow No. 5 color. He had found that some of his adult patients with asthmatic, gastrointestinal, and skin reactions had considerable benefit when placed on this special exclusion diet. When Dr. Feingold studied this diet, he was the first allergist to use it with children. When the children improved, he did not merely assume that the behavior improved because they felt better. He saw that these additives were somehow causally involved in the behavior problem itself. Clyde Hawley, MD, and I (1976) have reported that the sublingual drop testing of these children can select those children who will be helped by the diet. A sublingual drop test study of individual chemicals was published by Dr. Lockey in the *Annuals of Allergy* (1973). One can find dozens of papers about toxic responses to food additives in the medical literature.

The topic of nutrition has received little emphasis in medical research during the past thirty years. There has been a tendency to deal with it as if all of the facts had already been determined and that the job of the doctor was to place the person on a standardized diet. This attitude is particularly obvious when the topic of hypoglycemia is broached, for hypoglycemia is a complicated response in which at least eight factors participate. It often occurs because we eat too much refined flour and sugar; and when hypoglycemia occurs quickly it can cause a large number of diverse symptoms (Buckley 1969). The typical physician has an automatic "reflex" rejection of hypoglycemia as the cause of anything at all.

History of Medical Logic

This can be understood when we review the past history of medical logic about disease. Over a century ago there were discussions about the causes of disease. One group felt that several factors could add together to cause the disease, while another group preferred to consider just one agent responsible. The problem was "solved" by the discovery of germs as the cause of infection, and the unifactorial group had won. This group wants to insist that one factor will cause only one kind of response. This is not the case in regard to hypoglycemia. It has been found in adults that hypoglycemic disturbances range from epilepsy and headaches, through palpitation and peptic ulcers, to anxiety and exhaustion. The central nervous system center which is crucially involved in hypoglycemia is one which serves to regulate and inhibit centers and circuits which deal with several primary drives. These include foraging and feeding, and also fight-or-flight responses.

In hyperactive children these circuits are not being properly regulated, and the pathways of the ergotropic or sympathetic system are not properly inhibited. It has been proposed that this center in the hypothalamus is the one which is activated by stimulant drugs and which paradoxically helps the boy to be "safe and sane" rather than "fearless and foolish" (Buckley 1972).

Dr. Sieben has also failed to investigate the nutrition literature for experimental studies of the toxic effects of various organic chemicals. Several reports on the toxic effects of food additives have been published by Benjamin Ershoff of the Institute for Nutritional Studies in Culver City, California. He has developed a method for causing young, growing male rats to become quite sensitive to nutritional stress. These rats are placed on a fiber-free diet which satisfies all of the vitamin, mineral, and nutritional needs. He found that small amounts of certain additives would seriously damage or kill these rats. He could then add various kinds of fiber to the diet of other rats and protect them from the toxic response to these additives. Ershoff (1976) gave small amounts of FD and C Red No. 2, sodium cyclamate, or "Tween 60" to different groups of rats. They were not damaged when they received only one of these additives; but when all three chemicals were given to one group of rats, all were dead within two weeks. Food fiber was again found to have protective effects. This study shows that food additives can have additive or even synergistic toxic effects. In another study Ershoff (1977) has shown that sucrose can act like a food additive when used with cyclamate. In this study both groups of rats received 5 percent cyclamate. One group received their carbohydrate portion of the diet as cornstarch, and the other received sucrose. At the end of two weeks all rats receiving cornstarch had survived, and 10 of the 12 rats receiving sucrose as their only source of carbohydrate were dead.

This is not an experimental animal model for hyperkinesis. It is a biologic testing method which shows that certain qualities inherent in these chemicals have synergistic toxic effects when used by rats. They also show that it is ridiculous to demand to know which was the single factor responsible for death. The unifactorial infectious disease model does not apply to this disorder. There are several stresses which, together, combine to cause a disturbance which none of them alone would cause. Moreover, the demonstration that sucrose was dangerous to these rats supports (but does not prove) the proposals that watchful attention to nutrition can be of importance for the care of the disabled and the disordered.

My final comments will be obvious to any teacher. Dr. Sieben claims that there are two sorts of causes of learning disorders. One cause is social and educational, so that parents and teachers are probably at fault for damaging these children. This charge is reminiscent of perhaps the worst blunder in the history of psychiatry. There was no way that psychiatrists could find to account for the development of autism and childhood schizophrenic reactions. Instead of admitting honest ignorance, the profession accepted the proposal by Dr. Freda Fromm-Reichman that these children had been damaged by their "schizophrenogenic mothers." Almost thirty years have passed since this claim was made, and no pattern of communication has been shown to be unique to schizophrenia. On the contrary, adoption studies reveal that children from emotionally disturbed parents are the ones who become sick in their foster homes. These children do not learn schizophrenia from their parents or their schools. Nor do children learn to have learning disorders from their parents nor their teachers. The child will learn to express his disorder in ways that he learned from his family and his peers, but the cause of the disorder is organic.

Dr. Sieben has also proposed that there may be inherited genetic factors at work here. He does not dare to propose any helpful suggestions for those who raise and teach these children. Of course, he does suggest that these children should see a physician who could try to determine whether the child has some rare disease. He even offers us a list of disturbances which should be considered. This is called "differential diagnosis," and the one he provides is not useful at all.

Both hyperkinetic and learning disordered children have important organic components to their disturbance. They have a greater number of minor congenital anomalies than their well-adjusted siblings. The recent studies of mineral content of the hair demonstrated that the most disturbed children are much more likely to have high concentrations of lead in their hair. This is especially true for juvenile delinquents. So far, only the studies of toxic metals have given us valid findings which can be used in therapy. Some of these children have reactive hypoglycemia along with craving for candy, chocolate, and soft drinks. When they have refrained from any of these refined carbohydrates, several will begin to be "tuned up" by the Ritalin which they no longer need. The use of large amounts of vitamins, and of supplemental zinc, has been found to be of value for some seriously disordered children (Rimland 1974).

Conclusion

It has been proposed by Dr. Feingold and by Dr. Hawley and myself that there is a subgroup of hyperkinetic children who are sensitive to food additives. This subgroup has been estimated to consist of from one-third to one-half of the total number of hyperkinetic children. The well controlled double-blind study conducted by Dr. Conners does provide valid confirmation of this proposal. He dealt with the total group of 15 subjects as if all of them would be sensitive. This is the conservative way to use statistics because, if the subgroup of sensitive subjects is too small, a general statistic about the entire group will not confirm the existence of the subgroup. Dr. Conners wrote the paper which identified seven subgroups of hyperkinetic children, and it is regrettable that he did not comment about which subgroups were present in this dietary study.

It has also been proposed that the child who is sensitive to food additives must avoid all of them. The general assumption of physicians that there is only one cause for a disorder does not apply here.

Many of the compounds placed in food can have additive or synergistic effects to markedly increase the toxic response. This proposal is confirmed by the experiment in which Ershoff showed that the combination of two apparently benign additives caused marked toxicity and that three of them together killed the entire group of 12 rats.

The centers and circuits which deal with effective primary drive performance can become disordered by nutritional stress in some children. The junk food which these children are taught to seek through TV and other advertising can act in two ways to disturb brain function. The first instance is that the food contains none of the valuable components of organic food. These foods also contain several of the thousands of chemicals which can cause sensitivity reactions. Steven Lockey found that these can cause asthma, skin rashes, and headache in adults. Ben Feingold found that they can cause hyperkinesis in children. Rene Dubos, a biology professor emeritus of Rockefeller University, has skeptically concluded that man will probably never be able to adapt himself to " . . . the toxic effects of chemical pollution and of certain synthetic products, to the physiological and mental difficulties caused by lack of physical effort, to the mechanization of life, and to the presence of a wide variety of artificial stimulants" (1969).

References

Buckley, R. E. 1969. Hypoglycemic symptoms and the hypoglycemic experience. *Psychosomatics* 10:1 pp. 7-14.

Buckley, R. E. 1972. A neurophysiologic proposal for the amphetamine response in hyperkinetic children. *Psychosomatics* 13:2 pp. 93-99.

Buckley, R. E., and Gellhorn, E. 1969. Neurophysiological mechanisms underlying the action of hypo- and hyperglycemia in some clinical conditions. *Confinia Neurologica* 31:247-257.

Conners, C. K. 1973. Psychological assessment of children with minimal brain dysfunction. *Annals of the New York Academy of Science* 205:283-302.

Conners, C. K., et al. 1976. Food additives and hyperkinesis; a controlled double blind experiment. *Pediatrics* 58:154-156.

Dubos, R. 1969. World Health Assembly lecture, Human Ecology. Cited in Fishbein, M. 1970. Editorial. *Medical World News.*

Ershoff, B. H. 1976. Synergistic toxicity of food additives in rats fed a diet low in dietary fiber. *Journal of Food Science* 41:949-951.

Ershoff, B. H. 1977. Effects of dietary carbohydrates on sodium cyclamate toxicity in rats fed a purified, low fiber diet. *Proceedings of the Society for Experimental Biology and Medicine* 154:65-68.

Feingold, B. 1975. *Why your child is hyperactive.* New York: Random House.

Hawley, C., and Buckley, R. E. 1976. Hyperkinesis and sensitivity to the aniline food dyes. *Journal of Orthomolecular Psychiatry* 5:2 pp. 129-137.

Lockey, S. D. 1973. Drug reactions and sublingual testing with certified food colors. *Annals of Allergy* 31:9 pp. 423-429.

Rimland, B. 1974. An orthomolecular study of psychotic children. *Journal of Orthomolecular Psychiatry* 3:371-377.

Rimland, B.; Callaway, E.; and Dreyfus, P. 1977. The effect of high doses of vitamin B_6 on autistic children. *American Journal of Psychiatry.* In press.

The Effects of Caffeine on Hyperactive Children

Philip Firestone, PhD, Hélène Poitras-Wright, BA,
and Virginia Douglas, PhD

Philip Firestone, *educated at McGill University, is with the Psychology Department, Children's Hospital of Eastern Ontario and is associated with the Department of Psychology, Carleton University.* **Virginia I. Douglas** *is a professor in the Department of Psychology, McGill University and is a past president of the Canadian Psychological Association.* **Hélène Poitras-Wright**, *a graduate from McGill University, is currently completing her MA in clinical psychology at Concordia University.*

The voluminous research investigating the effects of stimulant drugs on hyperactive behavior is well known. Subsequent investigations into dietary influences are rapidly increasing in number, one such study to be published in an upcoming issue. This paper examines the effect of caffeine. Were these data to be replicable, avoiding the detrimental side effects of stimulant drugs among some children might be possible through the use of caffeine. — G.M.S.

The effects of a two-week regimen of caffeine on the behavior of hyperactive children were investigated. The double-blind study involved a crossover design and required each subject to be on caffeine and placebo for a period of two weeks. During this time, psychological, physiological, and behavioral observations were made. Caffeine did not significantly improve reaction times and psychological test scores. However, impulsivity and general behavior as measured by parent and teacher rating scales showed some significant improvements due to caffeine.

Hyperactivity is one of the difficult behavior management problems of children that is encountered by clinicians, and it has been estimated that 5% of all elementary-school children display this syndrome. Associated with high activity levels are several other symptoms, which include poor attention, low frustration tolerance, and impulsivity (Douglas 1974).

There is some disagreement as to the etiology of hyperactivity. Several researchers suggest that some type of organic malfunction is responsible (Douglas 1974), while others observe that child-rearing practices and reinforcement histories may also be implicated (Werry & Sprague 1969). Although early investigators speculated that hyperactive children outgrow the disorder, Douglas (1974) suggests that only the most obvious symptom, overactivity, disappears. Attention difficulties and impulse-control deficits, which may be central to the syndrome, seem to persist into adolescence (Weiss, Minde, Werry, Douglas, & Nemeth 1971).

2. HYPERACTIVE

Several investigators have implicated dysfunctions in arousal levels in the etiology of hyperactivity. Some have speculated that hyperactive children are overaroused and that stimulant drugs lower arousal level (Wender 1972), while others have suggested that these children are underaroused (Satterfield & Dawson 1971). Cohen and Douglas (1972) and, more recently, Spring, Greenberg, Scott, and Hopwood (1974) have found no differences between hyperactives and normals on resting skin conductance. To date, there seems to be no direct evidence to support the idea that the arousal level of hyperactives differs from that of normals.

During the last decade stimulant drugs (methylphenidate and the amphetamines) have emerged as the drugs of choice in the treatment of hyperactive children. Clinical studies (Sprague & Sleator 1973, Sroufe 1975) have suggested that the stimulants reduce restlessness, impulsivity, and distractibility and make activity more goal directed. A review of the studies using methylphenidate for hyperactivity reports an improvement in 70% to 90% of the children studied (Whalen & Henker 1976).

In spite of the positive effects of methylphenidate on various behaviors that make up the hyperactive syndrome, it has been estimated that 30% of those taking this medication develop annoying and sometimes serious side effects—these include loss of appetite, sleeplessness (Millichap & Fowler 1967), and depressive withdrawal (Douglas 1974). In addition, there are reports on the possibility of addiction (Sprague & Sleator 1973), potentially dangerous heart-rate changes (Cohen, Douglas, & Morgenstern 1971), and retardation in height and weight gain in children on chronic treatment with stimulants (Safer 1971).

Schnackenberg (1973) has suggested that caffeine may offer an alternative to the other stimulant drugs for some hyperactive children. In his private practice, he took 11 children who were responding with negative side effects off their Ritalin regimen and instructed their parents to substitute two cups of coffee per day. The children drank one cup of percolated or drip coffee in the morning and one at lunchtime. The total amount of caffeine ingested in one day was 250-300mg. Teachers, who reportedly did not know of this change in medication, were asked to fill out a questionnaire during the drug intervention, then while the children were on a medication holiday, then again while the children were receiving caffeine. Schnackenberg's data suggest that the children behaved as well on caffeine as on methylphenidate but that caffeine did not lead to negative side effects that were evident with the methylphenidate. Children behaved poorly when receiving neither of these substances.

Conners (1975)[*] also studied the effects of approximately 300mg caffeine on hyperactive children. In a double-blind crossover investigation, eight children were administered caffeine and placebo for three weeks each. Although the small number of children made statistical analysis impossible, Conners reports that there was no apparent advantage in favor of caffeine on five dependent measures (parent's observations, teacher's observations, continuous performance task, seat activity, and language test).

To date, two studies have compared the effects of caffeine and more traditional stimulant medication on the behavior of hyperactive children. Heustis, Arnold, and Smeltzer (1975) reported that hyperactive children (outpatients in a psychiatry clinic) improved significantly when D-amphetamine or methylphenidate was administered, but the improvement with caffeine was not statistically reliable. Eighty-milligram caffeine tablets were administered approximately three

---

[*] This paper was not published at the time of the present experiment, which was conducted in the spring of 1973.

times a day for a total of about 300mg per day for one week. Heustis et al. add a cautionary remark in relation to their results by suggesting that their small sample size (18 children) might have precluded the discovery of certain beneficial effects of caffeine. No negative side effects due to caffeine administration are reported.

Another study conducted with hyperactives in which caffeine and methylphenidate were compared also failed to find a significant clinical effect with caffeine (Garfinkel, Webster, & Sloman 1975). Garfinkel et al. compared 20mg methylphenidate and 160mg caffeine per day in their experiment, which had children on each drug for a 10-day period. The results indicated that methylphenidate was effective in controlling many aspects of the hyperactive syndrome but caffeine was not. However, this investigation did not constitute a realistic evaluation of the therapeutic effects of caffeine for several reasons. The small number of children studied (eight) and the fact that they were so unmanageable that hospital day care was required limits the generalization, which may not be useful for hyperactives normally seen in clinics or office practice.

In the present study an attempt was made to investigate more rigorously the effects of caffeine on hyperactivity. A double-blind crossover design was used with well-validated behavior-rating scales as well as psychological, physiological, and motor tests. In addition, a relatively large sample of hyperactives was used.

METHOD

Subjects. Twenty hyperactive male subjects were included, ranging in age from 5 yrs. 7 mos. to 12 yrs. 5 mos., with a mean of 9 yrs. 3 mos. (S D = 1.97). Their IQs ranged from 80 to 129 with a mean of 104.5 (S D = 10.78).

To select the subjects, teachers and principals were given a brief verbal description of the symptomatology characteristic of hyperactive children. This description focused mainly on three traits—overactivity, short attention span, and impulsivity. The teachers were then asked to fill out Conners' (1969) behavior rating scale for teachers. Children whose average score on the hyperactivity factor of the scale was 1.5 or greater were considered as candidates for the study. Further selection was based on parental interviews. For a child to be included, hyperactivity had to be chronic and present since early childhood. Excluded from the sample were children who showed definite signs of brain damage, epilepsy, or psychosis. None of the children were taking psychotropic medication, and all were living at home with at least one parent.

TESTS AND APPARATUS*

Psychological tests. Three psychological tests that have been shown sensitive to the therapeutic effects of amphetamines and methylphenidate were utilized: (1) the Matching Familiar Figures Test (MFF) (Campbell, Douglas, & Morgenstern 1971); (2) the Porteus Mazes Test (Conners, Taylor, Meo, Kurtz, & Fournier 1972), and (3) the Goodenough-Harris Draw-a-Person Test (Sroufe 1975). Conners' 10-point rating scale (Conners et al. 1972) and Davids' 7-point scale (Davids 1971) were filled out by parents and teachers in order to assess children's behavior.

Delayed reaction time apparatus. The delayed reaction time (DRT) apparatus has been used previously and has been shown to discriminate between normal and hyperactive subjects in addition to being sensitive to the

---

* A more comprehensive version of the tests and apparatus may be found in Firestone and Douglas (1975).

effects of methylphenidate (Cohen, Douglas, & Morgenstern 1971). The DRT apparatus was triggered by auditory stimuli that had been preprogrammed. Onset of the warning signal (WS) marked the beginning of a 10-second preparatory interval after which a reaction signal (RS) was activated, while trials were separated by a 5-second interval.

While performing on the DRT, the subjects were to release the reaction time button only to the RS. However, it soon became evident that they were making three kinds of inappropriate "impulsive" responses. *False starts* refers to those button releases that occurred between the onset of the WS and up to 2.5 seconds following its occurrence. *Interstimulus responses* were those that occurred from 2.5 seconds after the WS up to the onset of the RS. Responses after the button release to the RS occurring before the WS of the next trial were designated *redundant responses*.

Skin conductance. A Grass Model 17 polygraph was used to make continuous recordings of skin conductance. Tonic skin conductance readings were taken at 30-second intervals during the last 5 minutes of the 10-minute relaxation period and at the moment of WS onset during the DRT. Skin conductance changes in excess of .30 μmho were counted as phasic responses. A skin conductance orienting response (OR) was scored if it occurred within .5–4.0 seconds of the WS onset. On the same trials skin conductance responses that occurred 2.5 or fewer seconds prior to the RS were considered as anticipatory skin conductance responses (ASR), while a skin conductance response following the RS, from .5–4.0 seconds, was designated as the reaction response (RR).

PROCEDURE

All children included in the caffeine study were given a physical examination by a physician. A double-blind crossover technique was used so that each subject served as his own control. Caffeine and placebo tablets were coded by a psychologist who did none of the testing. The caffeine tablets, which were indistinguishable from the placebos, contained 150mg of caffeine. The order in which active drug and placebo were administered was randomized so that half the subjects were first treated with caffeine, then with placebo; for the other half the reverse order was used. Parents were instructed to give the children one tablet every morning before school as well as on Saturday and Sunday. The children also took a tablet at lunchtime every day. An experimenter telephoned the parents every two days to ensure that the instructions were carried out. For those subjects (about half the sample) who did not go home for lunch, a teacher at each school was in charge of dispensing tablets.

The time covered by the study included a two-week period during which children were on caffeine or placebo, followed by one week when they received no medication and another two-week period during which they received either caffeine or placebo.

General testing procedures. Each child was tested 14 days after starting the caffeine or placebo regimen. On the day of the testing subjects took their tablets exactly one hour before testing began. One experimenter administered the Porteus Mazes, the MFF, and the Draw-a-Person Test and another the DRT. The paper-and-pencil tests were always administered first, in an empty office, and their order of presentation was randomized among subjects. The DRT was administered last. The psychological tests took approximately 25 minutes; the DRT lasted about 20 minutes.

The physical setting for the DRT consisted of a small windowless room isolated in the basement of an elementary school and kept at a temperature of approximately 70° F. The room was divided by a large plywood screen that contained a one-way mirror. The subject was seated alone on one side of the screen while the polygraph, tape recorder, and programming equipment were operated by the experimenter on the other side.

The subject was seated in a semireclining chair and told that the experimenter was interested in how well he could pay attention to things, and the electrodes were then placed on two fingers of his left hand. He was told that when the experiment started he was to keep the response button down. When he heard a beep through the earphones, it meant he should get ready because the light was going to come on. When the light came on, he was to let go of the button as quickly as possible so we could see how fast he was. Then he was to depress the button again and hold it until the next time a light came on.

Before the experiment started, the subject was put through a 10-minute relaxation period in order that skin conductance might stabilize.

Behavior rating scales. On day 7 and on day 14, the days on which each child was tested, one of the experimenters telephoned the parents and asked the mother to fill out the previously supplied rating scales and return them by mail. On the same day the same experimenter visited the child's teachers and picked up the two rating scales. Behavior ratings were thus collected every seven days during drug or placebo consumption. No ratings were collected during the one-week "off" period, as this was a vacation period at the schools attended by the children.

DATA ANALYSIS

Statistical transformation: autonomic data. In order to account for the nonnormality of the distribution often found in autonomic data and also to account for the Law of Initial Values, it was necessary to perform a transformation on the raw data. Skin conductance values were converted to log scores, and all

skin conductance changes were expressed as the difference between the logarithm of the base and peak of the response to stimulation.

Missing data. Due to illness and absenteeism on the part of the teachers and students, there were a few subjects for whom observational data (rating scales) were lacking. If the missing data for a subject covered only one observation, a score was estimated using Winer's (1962, pp. 488-489) estimation procedure; if two observations were missing, the subject was dropped from that analysis. As a result, although there were data for 20 subjects on the DRT and psychological tests, only 14 subjects met the criteria for inclusion in the observational analyses.

RESULTS

All data were analysed by analysis of variance. Significant main effects were followed by the Neuman-Keuls test.

Performance on the Delayed Reaction Time Task

Reaction Times. A two-way analysis of variance was conducted on both mean reaction times and the standard deviation of the reaction times. The two factors were drug (caffeine vs. placebo) and order. There were no significant findings on either (see Table I).

Impulsive responses. The analysis of variance of the false starts resulted in a significant drug effect ($F = 9.2$, $df = 2/36$, $p < .01$). As Table I indicates, this showed that false starts were more numerous with placebo than with caffeine. Although there appeared to be fewer interstimulus and redundant responses in the caffeine condition, the analyses did not produce significant differences.

Autonomic activity during the DRT. A three-way analysis of variance on tonic skin conductance with drug, order, and condition

TABLE I. *Performance on the delayed reaction time task in the caffeine and placebo conditions.*

	Caffeine	Placebo
Mean reaction time	38.88	41.36
Standard deviation of reaction time	17.35	19.52
False starts	.70	1.90*
	(1.00)†	(1.37)
Interstimulus responses	1.65	2.20
	(2.49)	(2.52)
Redundant responses	1.25	2.35
	(2.21)	(2.24)

* p < .05.   † Standard deviations are in parentheses.

TABLE II. *Effects of caffeine and placebo on psychological test scores.*

	Pretest	Caffeine	Placebo
Porteus Mazes Test	108.40	126.90	123.25
	(30.92)*	(10.36)	(39.56)
Draw-a-Person Test	85.45	97.05	92.60
	(13.06)	(18.65)	(11.62)
Matching Familiar Figures Test			
Latency	7.95	7.00	7.50
	(3.25)	(2.90)	(2.65)
Error	15.40	14.30	14.90
	(7.79)	(6.02)	(5.53)

* Standard deviations are in parentheses.

(rest or performance phase) as main effects was carried out. The only significant finding ($F = 16.3$, $df = 1/18$, $p < .01$) revealed that tonic skin conductance was lower in the rest condition than while the subjects were performing on the DRT (31.8 μmho vs. 37.1 μmho).

The analyses on the amplitude and frequency of the phasic skin conductance responses yielded no significant effects.

Performance on the Psychological Tests. Performance on the psychological tests (Table II) was evaluated three times: just before the subject began taking caffeine,

while they were on caffeine, and in the placebo condition. A two-way analysis of variance of the MFF for both latency and errors yielded no significant effects.

The analysis of the Porteus Mazes scores yielded a significant time effect ($F = 20.8$, $df = 2/36$, $p < .001$). This difference reflects a practice effect only; no treatment effect was evident.

The analysis of variance on the Draw-a-Person Test also revealed a significant time effect ($F = 8.1$, $df = 2/36$, $p < .01$). This indicated that performance in the pretest was reliably poorer than in both the caffeine (Q

= 9.7, $df = 17$, $p < .01$) and placebo trials ($Q = 8.4$, $df = 17$, $p < .05$). No significant treatment differences were found.

Teachers' Ratings

The two-way analysis of variance on the teachers' ratings from the Davids' scale yielded no significant effects (Table III). A similar analysis of the Conners teachers' ratings resulted in a significant drug effect ($F = 5.5$, $df = 4/48$, $p < .01$). Scores on the pretest were reliably higher than on observations in the caffeine 2 condition, but not significantly different from scores in caffeine 1 ($Q = 4.6$, $df = 15$, $p < .05$). In addition, the first and second ratings with caffeine were reliably lower than the first rating in the placebo condition ($Q = 4.6$, $df = 15$, $p < .05$; $Q = 5.22$, $df = 15$, $p < .05$), but not different from the second rating in the placebo condition.

Parents' Rating

The two-way analysis of variance on the Davids' scale (Table III) did not produce any significant findings. The Conners rating scale showed a significant drug effect ($F = 9.8$, $df = 4/48$, $p < .01$), indicating that pretest scores were higher than scores at the time of both caffeine and the placebo 1 ratings ($Q = 5.66$, $df = 15$, $p < .01$; $Q = 6.14$, $df = 15$, $p < .01$; $Q = 4.88$, $df = 15$, $p < .01$). Both ratings when the subjects were receiving caffeine were significantly lower than those made during the placebo 2 condition ($Q = 4.8$, $df = 15$, $p < .05$; $Q = 5.18$, $df = 15$, $p < .05$).

DISCUSSION

Although the findings are not consistent, the change effected by 300mg caffeine per day in the present study is not as dramatic as that reported by Schnackenberg (1975). The means and variability of reaction times on the DRT seemed better in the caffeine than the placebo condition, but the differences were not significant. Baker and Theologus (1972) speculated that caffeine serves to improve performance on attention tasks by retarding deterioration over time. It could be argued that the 15 trials of the DRT in the present study, which took only three to four minutes, might not have been long enough for a significant difference to appear. In those studies that have demonstrated the positive effects of methylphenidate on the delayed reaction time task (Cohen, Douglas, & Morgenstern 1971) and on a vigilance task (Sykes, Douglas, & Morgenstern 1972), subjects were required to participate for a considerably greater length of time.

The effect of caffeine on the ability to inhibit responses remains unclear. Although the frequency of false starts was significantly lower in the caffeine condition, interstimulus, redundant responses and psychological test scores (i.e., MFF, Porteus Mazes, Draw-a-Person) do not support this finding.

Some studies have found heightened skin conductance levels with stimulant drugs (Satterfield & Dawson 1971; Cohen et al. 1971), while others have not (Spring et al. 1974). Spring et al. have suggested that differences in dosage levels may have accounted for the fact that their hyperactive subjects did not show increases in tonic skin conductance while those of Cohen et al. (1971) did. In the present study, caffeine did not appreciably raise tonic levels (32.9 μmho to 35.9 μmho). Whether higher dosages or more prolonged use of caffeine would affect skin conductance remains to be seen. The data raise hope, however, that detrimental autonomic side effects sometimes found with the stimulants (Douglas 1974, Sroufe 1975) may not occur with caffeine. As in the previously reported studies with caffeine, the children in this study did not show any negative side effects, as determined by informal parental reports.

TABLE III. *Means and standard deviations of teacher and parent rating scales scores.*

		Pre	Caffeine		Placebo	
			1	2	1	2
Teachers						
Davids' rating scale	Mean	24.50	25.14	23.07	25.15	24.93
	SD	11.28	5.01	8.53	8.06	3.64
Conners' short form rating scale	Mean	17.36	12.86°†	12.15°†	17.92	14.22
	SD	8.97	6.67	6.05	6.10	9.94
Parents						
Davids' rating scale	Mean	26.08	21.79	21.22	23.21	26.07
	SD	5.52	6.98	7.89	7.53	3.81
Conners' short form rating scale	Mean	17.07	9.79°†	9.79°‡	11.50°	13.93
	SD	8.65	6.63	8.07	7.05	6.05

* Significantly lower than pre scores.
† Significantly lower than ratings obtained during the first placebo trial.
‡ Significantly lower than ratings obtained during the second placebo trial.

Caffeine induced significant effects on ratings of classroom and home behavior. Conners' 10-point rating scale showed its sensitivity to caffeine as it has to other stimulants (Sprague & Sleator 1973). Both teachers and parents indicated that caffeine may well increase the frequency of desirable behaviors in hyperactive children, although this change, in the present investigation, was inconsistent. Davids' scale did not show any significant changes, though the scores were in the direction of caffeine improving behavior.

Significant effects with caffeine leading to improved performance were found on three measures: false starts, and Conners' rating scale as filled out by parents and by teachers. All other dependent measures utilized showed nonsignificant differences in the same direction (e.g., MFF, Porteus Mazes, Draw-a-Person, reaction time and its variability, Davids' rating scale by teachers and parents). The reasons for this are not clear, but some speculation is warranted. It is possible that the small number of subjects or their variable ages and IQs may have precluded more definite results. In addition, as suggested by Conners (1975), 300mg caffeine may be too conservative a dose for any substantial behavior change. This is supported by the lack of side effects in the children in this study and the Conners study. Furthermore, it is possible that only certain children are caffeine responders, as is the case with other stimulants.

"The Hyperkinetic Child: Some Consensually Validated Behavioral Corrolates"

by Jules Schrager, Director, Department of Social Work
                University Hospital
    Janet Lindy, Research Assistant
    Saul Harrison, Associate Professor
    John Mc Dermott, Assistant Professor
    Elizabeth Killins, Social Worker, University Michigan.
                Medical Center, Ann Arbor

The mere mention of the term "hyperkinetic syndrome" is guaranteed to raise eyebrows in medical, psychological, and educational circles. Although the literature is rife with references to this phenomenon, there is, nonetheless, disagreement concerning its implication for diagnostic appraisal and treatment. The variety of phrases used to describe what is essentially the same symptom complex underlines the lack of concensus.

Against a background of discrepancy, a survey was undertaken among a number of disciplines concerned with the hyperkinetic child. This was part of a larger study involving screening of 500 children admitted to kindergarten in September of 1964 in six Ann Arbor public schools. A behavioral checklist containing 55 items was completed by 23 teachers, 13 psychologists, 16 psychiatrists, 15 social workers, and 12 pediatricians. The instructions given to the respondents were as follows:

Definition- we are employing the term "hyperkinetic syndrome" in this study although others use such terms as "emotionally immature" "minimally brain-damaged," "anxious", "Strauss syndrome," or ""organically driven" to describe essentially similar children. The following List of Behaviors or symptoms contains within it those which are particularly relevant to a diagnosis of this disorder, others which are less so, and some which seem to have no relevance at all. Place the number (1) next to those you think are particularly relevant; the number (2) next to those you think less relevant; the number (3) next to those you think have no relevance at all. *Then select those six behaviors you think are most significant* to your designation of a child who presents the hyperkinetic syndrome.

Table 1 indicates those items checked by the five professional groups in the survey. A double asterisk indicates that 75 percent or more of the sample have rated item number (1) most significant. Where one asterisk appears, the item has been rated number (1) by at least 50 percent of the sample.

Despite the ambiguity surrounding the hyperkinetic syndrome, good interdisciplinary agreement is observed concerning its behavioral characteristics. Seventy-five percent or more of all groups felt the following six behaviors to be primary:

1. figets and restless
2. inattentive,
3. hard to manage
4. can't sit still
5. easily distracted
6. low frustration

Medical professionals were concerned also with irritability, undisciplined, clumsy, poor sleeper, seems slow, and awkward.

Reprinted from *Exceptional Children,* May 1966. ©1966 Council for Exceptional Children.

2. HYPERACTIVE

Hyperkinetic children have been studied under various rubrics. They are brought to the helping professionals because they are a disruptive influence in the home, are poor students, and are difficult to manage in most situations. Various educational, psychotherapeutic, and pharmacologic approaches have been tried. Questions arise repeatedly as to the group's homogeneity. Although differences appear as to etiology and to the meaning of symptoms, there is high order of agreement as to the significant signs and symptoms. Whether the hyperkinetic child is a project of insult to the brain, disturbed intrafamilial relations, poor genetic composition, or a consequence of overwhelming social pressures is equivocal. Information concerning consensually validated behavioral attributes of these children can serve as an aid in identifying the group to be studied further. It should lead also to the development of new intervention strategies which might be employed in order to enable these children to move less eventfully through the school room experiences.

TABLE 1

Behavior of Hyperkinetic Children as Rated by Five Professional Groups

	Pediatricians N=12	Teachers N=23	Psychologists N=13	Psychiatrists N=16	Social Workers N=15
Fidgets, Restless	**	**	**	**	**
Inattentive	**	**	**	**	**
Hard to Manage	**	**	**	**	**
Can't Sit Still	**	**	**	**	**
Easily Distracted	**	**	**	**	**
Can't Take Frustration	**	**	**	**	**
Anxiety		**	*	**	**
No Self Control	**	**	*	**	**
Breaks Things Impulsively			*	**	**
Nervous	**	*	*	**	*
Irritable	**			**	
Undisciplined	*			**	
Clumsy	**				
Poor Sleeper				*	
Seems Slow	**				
Awkward	**				

****

May 1966 Exceptional Children

Hyperkinesis and Learning Disabilities linked to the Ingestion of Artifical Food Colors and flavors

Ben F. Feingold, MD

The epidemic of encephalitis that occurred during World War I left in its wake a number of cases with true brain damage characterized by signs and symptoms that are now identified with hyperkinesis. Following the collation of the clinical experience of this period by Cohen and Kahn in 1934, it became common practice to label all patients presenting a similar clinical pattern as having brain damage (BD). Abetted by the reports of Strauss and his collaborators (Strauss & Lehtinen 1948, Money 1962, Strauss & Kephart 1955), the practice of labeling individuals as organically brain damaged without adequate substantiating evidence continued into the 1950s.

In the early 1960s, to mitigate the stigma associated with the diagnosis of brain damage, the word "minimal" was introduced. Later the diagnostic term was further tempered by substituting "dysfunction" for "damage"; this led to the commonly encountered term, "minimal brain dysfunction." In 1957 Laufer and Denhoff suggested the term "hyperkinetic

<table>
<tr><td colspan="2">TABLE I. Etiologies in neurologic damage.</td></tr>
<tr><td colspan="2">During Pregnancy</td></tr>
<tr><td></td><td>Toxemia of mother (eclampsia)</td></tr>
<tr><td></td><td>Hemorrhage</td></tr>
<tr><td></td><td>Infection</td></tr>
<tr><td></td><td>Drugs</td></tr>
<tr><td></td><td>Environmental toxicants (air, food, water)</td></tr>
<tr><td colspan="2">During Delivery</td></tr>
<tr><td></td><td>Anesthsia</td></tr>
<tr><td></td><td>Trauma</td></tr>
<tr><td colspan="2">Post Partum</td></tr>
<tr><td></td><td>Respiratory distress</td></tr>
<tr><td></td><td>Jaundice</td></tr>
<tr><td></td><td>Infection</td></tr>
<tr><td></td><td>Environmental toxicants.</td></tr>
</table>

impulse disorder" which, through usage, has been abbreviated to "hyperkinesis" and frequently to "hyperactivity."

During the last 50 years, a considerable literature has accumulated which reports attempts to categorize the kaleidoscope of signs and symptoms representing this condition into specific clinical entities (Bax & MacKeith 1963). Depending upon the orientation of the observer and the dominant characteristic presented when the patient was examined, numerous labels were invented for variations of the identical problem (Clements 1966). Many times the descriptive classification carried with it a proposal for treatment and management, as well as hypotheses suggesting the etiology or underlying biological disorder.

A number of etiologies have been proposed for hyperkinesis (see Table I). Causal factors include toxemia, hemorrhage, and drugs during pregnancy; anesthesia causing asphyxia neonatorum and trauma during delivery; psychological and emotional factors; environmental pollutants of the air, water, and food supply.

One of the most widespread and critically important, yet not fully recognized, group of pollutants in the environment is food additives. Food additives may be classified as intentional or nonintentional. Nonintentional food additives are the chemicals and substances that accidently gain entrance into the food supply — e.g., insect parts; animal hairs and feces; soil, water, and air pollutants; packaging materials, etc. Intentional additives represent the chemicals that are deliberately introduced into the food supply for specific functions or purposes.

The classification of intentional food additives in Table II lists 13 categories consisting of 2,764 compounds compiled from data gathered by the National Science Foundation in 1965. This is not a complete list. The precise number of intentional additives may approach 3,800 or even 4,000. The exact number is not known.

Of all additives introduced into foods, synthetic colors and flavors are perhaps the most common. By virtue of this, synthetic colors and flavors are the most common cause of adverse reactions, affecting practically every system of the body (Table III). It is because of this comparatively high frequency of reactions attributed to the added colors and flavors that we have focused our attention upon these two classes of additives. This does not imply that the remaining categories do not cause adverse reactions. No chemical is exempt, since any compound in existence, whether natural or synthetic, may induce an adverse reaction if its consumer has the appropriate genetic profile, i.e., predisposition. This being true, it becomes essential to evaluate each compound or class of compounds for its benefit compared with the risk associated with its use.

In addition to being the most common cause of adverse reactions, the synthetic colors and flavors have no nutritional value. Their function is purely cosmetic, so that deleting them from the food supply would cause no significant loss. Accordingly, on balance, the risk associated with synthetic colors and flavors outweighs their benefits.

Of all observed reactions to such compounds, perhaps the most dramatic and most critical are the behavioral disturbances. Initially, it may be surprising that food additives can cause behavioral disturbances. Closer analysis allays surprise. Except for terminology, there is no difference between certain compounds when they are used as medicines or when they are introduced into foods as additives. Both are low molecular weight compounds. The availability of behavior-modifying drugs is common knowledge. There are drugs that stimulate, drugs that depress, and others that modify the subject's mood. It is not remarkable that among the thousands of additives in the food supply there may be compounds with similar effects upon behavioral and emotional patterns.

It is surprising indeed to recognize that none of the thousands of chemicals introduced into food as additives has ever been subjected to pharmacological studies such as those that are required for a compound before it can be licensed for use as a drug (Schmidt 1975). Certainly, there is little knowledge of the behavioral toxicology of these additives.

The patient who first attracted my attention to the possibility of a link between behavioral disturbances and the ingestion of artificial food colors and flavors was a 40-year-old woman who reported to the Allergy Department because of angioedema of the face and periorbital region (Feingold 1973). Her food intake was restricted according to the K-P Diet (Table IV) and her angioedema cleared. During the initial interview, the patient had failed to report that she had been in psychotherapy for two years

TABLE II. Classification of international additives°

Preservatives	33
Antioxidants	28
Sequestrants	45
Surface active agents	111
Stabilizers, thickener	39
Bleaching and maturing agents	24
Buffers, acids, alkalies	60
Food colors	34
Nonnutritive and special dieatry sweetners	4
Nutritive supplement	117
Flavoring-synthetic	1610
Flavoring-natural	502
Miscellaneous: yeast foods,texturizers,firming agents,binders,anticaking agents,enzymes	157
Total number of additives	2764

°Compiled from data gathered by the National Sceince Foundation in 1965

because of a behavioral disturbance characterized by hostility toward her husband, inability to socialize with her peers, and conflict with her coworkers. While she adhered to the K-P Diet, her behavior improved. She also noted that any infraction of the diet induced an immediate recurrence of both the angioedema and the disturbed behavioral pattern.

Having been alerted to a possible link between food additives and behavior, we observed other adults with a similar association, and also children with the apparent same relationship. Since the children were reporting to the Allergy Department, their primary complaints were somatic — e.g., pruritus, urticaria, angioedema, localized skin lesions, nasal symptoms, and at times gastrointestinal complaints. Early in the course of these observations, none of the parents volunteered information that a child was experiencing behavioral disturbances, often associated with problems at school. After the K-P Diet was ordered for

TABLE III. Adverse reactions induced by flavors and colors.

1. Respiratory
   Rhinitis
   Nasal polyps
   Cough
   Laryngeal edema
   Hoarseness (laryngeal nodes)
   Asthma
2. Skin
   Pruritus
   Dermatographia
   Localized skin lesions
   Urticaria
   Angioedema
3. Gastrointestinal
   Macroglossia
   Flatulence and pyrosis
   Constipation
   Buccal chancres
4. Neurological Symptoms
   Headaches
   Behavioral disturbances
5. Skeletal System
   Arthralgia with edema

treatment of the physical complaint, the parents would report not only control of the physical problem, but also a marked change in the child's behavioral pattern (Feingold 1975).

To test whether the observations of the parents would be confirmed, we arranged for management by the K-P Diet of children whose primary complaint was a behavioral disturbance, usually labeled MBD or hyperkinesis. Using the Conners Rating Scale (Conners 1969), ratings were made prior to the initial visit and periodically following dietary management, initially at 2-week and then at 4-week intervals. We were soon able to confirm the parents' earlier reports. Children with a history of signs and symptoms* usually leading to a diagnosis of MBD or hyperkinesis, when managed with the K-P Diet, experienced a marked change in behavioral pattern within 3 to 21 days, depending upon the age of the child. Children who had been receiving various behavior-modifying drugs could discontinue these agents, while the behavioral pattern continued to improve. When rated by teachers on a quarterly or semester basis, children who had had difficulty at school showed a marked adjustment to the classroom environment and rapid improvement in scholastic achievement. Any dietary challenge, inadvertent or deliberate, induced a recurrence of the behavioral disturbance which persisted for 24 hours to four days, so that a child experiencing an infraction only twice a week could have a persistence of the clinical pattern.

A double-blind crossover study funded by the National Institute of Education and directed by Dr. C. Keith Conners of the University of Pittsburgh (Conners, Goyette, Southwick, Lees, & Andrulonis 1976) has confirmed that dietary management favorably influences hyperactivity at the .005 level of significance on a teacher-rating scale and at .05 on a parent-rating scale. The subjects of this study initially

*The history developed at the initial visit covered all developmental periods -- prenatal, perinatal, infancy, nursery school, kindergarten, elementary and secondary school. For older patients, performance before and after puberty was stressed.

comprised 57 children who were reviewed in advance of the investigation. Through attrition, chiefly failure to comply with the structure of the study, the group was finally reduced to 15 children who fulfilled all the requirements of the protocol. Five of the 15 children demonstrated unequivocally that dietary management influenced hyperactivity as long as there was full compliance with the diet. Any infraction or challenge was followed within hours by a recurrence of the behavioral pattern.

The Food Research Institute (1976) of the University of Wisconsin conducted a double-blind crossover study on 36 boys of school age (6 to 12 years) and 10 children who were three to five years of age. In the school age group, four children in the sample showed significant improvement as rated by both parents and teachers and/or on several of the objective measures employed. The younger children (age 3 to 5) showed a greater positive response to the experimental diet as indicated by parent rating. All ten mothers in this group rated their child's behavior as improved as did four of the seven fathers in this sample.

The numerous variables of the hyperkinetic syndrome coupled with the many environmental variables do not permit valid statistical conclusions on the basis of the short-term, segmental observations employed in both the Conners and the Wisconsin study. These studies merely confirmed that the K-P Diet influences behavior.

All our clinical observations have been replicated in a pilot clinical study (Cook & Woodhill 1976) in Australia, directed by a psychiatrist with the Sydney Ministry of Health, and the chairperson of Prince Henry Hospital's Department of Nutrition at Little Bay, New South Wales.

Both the Department of Health, Education, and Welfare in this country and the Medical Research Council of Australia are funding further studies of the problem.

RESPONSES TO MANAGEMENT WITH THE K-P DIET

Five separate programs, representing a total of 360 children managed with the K-P Diet, showed favorable responses ranging from 30 to 50% of the sample, depending upon the mean age of the children and the presence or absence of a history suggestive of neurologic damage. Precise determination for the percentage of responders to dietary management will require large samples, perhaps 1,000 subjects or more, studied longitudinally over a period of several years. At this level, it is important to recognize that dietary intervention does influence the behavioral deficits of the hyperkinetic syndrome and, particularly, hyperactivity.

All of the deficits associated with the hyperkinetic or MBD syndrome listed in Table V are not observed in every child. Not only does each child have his own mosaic of deficits, but for any given child, the pattern may vary from day to day, and at times even from hour to hour. Hyperactivity is usually the dominant feature

Learning Disabilities

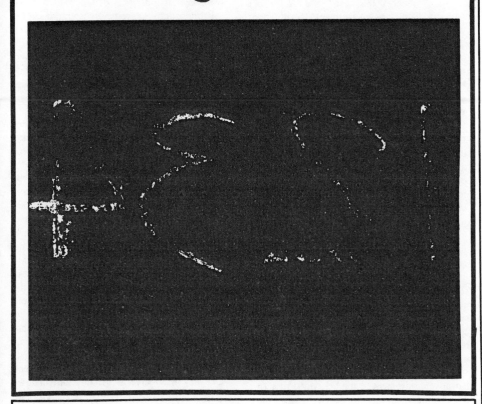

TABLE IV. The Kaiser-Permanente (K-P) Diet.

Omit the following, as indicated:

1. Foods containing natural salicylates

Almonds	Mint flavors
Apples (cider & cider vinegars)	Nectarines
Apricots	Oranges
Blackberries	Peaches
Cherries	Plums or prunes
Cloves	Raspberries
Cucumbers and pickles	Strawberries
Currants	All tea
Gooseberries	Tomatoes
Grapes or raisins (wines & wine vinegars)	Oil of wintergreen

The salicylate-containing foods may be restored following 4 to 6 weeks of favorable response provided no history of aspirin sensitivity exists in the family.

II. All foods that contain artificial colors and flavors

III. Miscellaneous items

All aspirin-containing compounds
All medications with artificial colors and flavors
Toothpaste and toothpowder (substitute salt and soda or unscented Neutrogena soap)
All perfumes

Note: Check all labels of food items and drugs for artificial coloring and flavoring. Since permissible foods without artificial colors and flavors vary from region to region, it is not practical to compile a list of permissible foods. Each individual must learn to read the ingredients on the label. When added colors and flavors are specified, the item is prohibited. If in doubt, the food should not be used. Instead, it is advisable to prepare the substitute at home from scratch.

TABLE V. Descriptive characteristics of clinical pattern of H-DL

GROUP I

Marked Hyperactivity and Fidgetness
Constant motion

Rocks and jiggles legs
Dances, and wiggles hands
Runs, does not walk

in infancy, crib rocking, head knocking, fretfulness
Compulsive Aggression
Disruptive at home and at school
Compulsively touches everything and everyone
Disturbes other children
Perseverates-cannot be diverted from an action even when life threatening

Excitable-Impulsive
Behavior is unpredictble
Panics easily
Frustration leading to temper tantrum

No Patience
Low tolerance for failure and frustration
Demands must be met immediately

Short Attention Span
Unable to concentrate

Poor Sleep Habits
Diffcult to get to bed
Hard to fall asleep
Easily awakened

GROUP II

Gross Muscle Incoordination
Exceptionally clumsy
Trips when walking
Collides with objects
Cannot function in sports
Cannot bicycle or swim

Fine Muscle Incoordination
Eyes and hands do not seem to operate together
Difficulty with: Buttoning and tying
writing and drwaing
speech-stuttering
reading-dyslexia

GROUP III

Cognitive and Perceptive Disturbances
Auditory and memory deficits
Visual memory deficits
Deficits in understanding
Difficulty in reasoning, e.g. a math problem
Normal or high I.Q. but fails at school

Boys involved 7:1

Rarely more than one child in a family affected

2. HYPERACTIVE

of the pattern, but it is not always present. One child may exhibit features of only a single group listed in Table V; in other children, various combinations of deficits drawn from one or more of the three groups may characterize the behavioral pattern. At times only a single deficit may be observed. However, if this deficit is a critical one – e.g., an auditory perceptual or a visual perceptual disturbance – severe learning disabilities may result.

Although we have observed the response to dietary management for five years, we are still unable to predict from history, physical examination, and neurologic and psychometric tests the ultimate response of the individual. Similarly, assumptions regarding the speed and degree of response to dietary management cannot be made on the basis of estimates of neurologic damage, previous use of medicines, or age of the child. Children with a history suggesting a possible cause for neurologic damage may experience a complete recovery on the diet, while others with a completely negative history may fail to respond, or may show a partial response, such as improved behavior with deficits in coordination, or cognition, or perception. The history cannot always be precise in disclosing neurotoxic factors. Not infrequently the mother, relying upon memory, cannot accurately reconstruct the events before or during pregnancy. In addition, consideration must be given to less overt factors, such as environmental pollutants of air, soil, and water, which serve as neurobehavioral toxicants during gestation or early childhood.

A determination can be made only through strict application of the diet.

When a favorable response follows dietary management, the initial improvement is in the behavioral pattern (Table V, Group I). Control of aggression, impulsiveness, and the tendency to perseverate results in a calmer child; the improvement in mood enables the child to concentrate, which leads to improved attention. If there are no cognitive or perceptual deficits, there is rapid improvement in learning. The child who was abusive, disobedient, incorrigible, and disdainful of attention moves toward becoming affectionate, lovable, and responsive to guidance.

Correction of the behavioral pattern may be followed rapidly by improved muscular coordination (Table V, Group II). Improvement of the gross muscle involvement corrects awkwardness in gait and permits participation in sports, such as swimming, ball games, and bicycle riding. Improvement of the fine muscle coordination leads to improved writing and drawing skills and, in some children, improved speech.

Cognition and perception (Table V, Group III) are next to respond; improvement in these permits increased scholastic achievement. Learning ability may show a slow improvement over months or even years. An improved behavioral pattern always precedes the correction

in coordination, cognition, and perception. The latter deficits do not improve unless behavior responds to the diet. Cognitive and perceptual deficits are those that persist most commonly, causing learning disabilities even after a marked improvement in behavior and muscle coordination.

Age influences the speed and degree of response to dietary management. Usually, the younger the child, the more rapid and more complete the response. In early infancy improvement or reversal of all signs and symptoms may occur within 24 to 48 hours after elimination of pediatric vitamin drops, a rich source of synthetic colors and flavors. The two- to five-year-old child may improve after five days, while the five- to 12-year-old child may respond in 10 to 14 days. In some children, particularly those who have received long-acting drugs, e.g., dextroamphetamine Spansules® or large doses of behavior-modifying drugs [amphetamine, methylphenidate (Ritalin®), Stelazine®, Mellaril®, Tofranil®, Elavil®, Vistaril®, Cylert®], the response may be delayed for 3 to 5 weeks. Very often, following such delays the improvement may occur abruptly rather than develop gradually.

The older child, postpubescent or adolescent, usually requires a longer period, frequently several months, before improvement is noted; even then, the response is not always complete. The highest incidence of failure to respond to dietary management is observed among patients treated during adolescence.

As the child passes through puberty, a spontaneous improvement in the behavioral pattern may be observed. If the deficits persist, the adolescent cannot perform to his full potential. This makes it difficult for him to cope with his environment, leading to frustration resulting in withdrawal, antisocial behavior, lying, stealing, and ultimately, in many cases, juvenile delinquency.

BEHAVIORAL TOXICOLOGY

The behavioral disturbances with learning disabilities attributed to the ingestion of artificial food colors and flavors represent a small band in the broad spectrum of the newly emerging discipline of behavioral toxicology. Accordingly, the variety of clinical patterns observed can best be interpreted relative to some considerations that are basic to this discipline.

Since molecules of almost any substance can cross the placental barrier, it must be recognized that any environmental compound, whether ingested, inhaled, or injected, has the potential of being toxic to the fetus. The developing organism does not have the same capacity as a fully developed person to metabolize and detoxify potentially toxic substances. Accordingly, the fetus, particularly during the stage of organ differentiation, is highly susceptible to the insults of any sub-

stance crossing the placental barrier.

The teratogenic damage which may be manifest as either overt or covert alterations in the organism is governed by the genetic profile of the individual, the nature and doses of the offending compound, and the stage of organ development at the time of the insult. It is conceivable that substances of low toxicity or in small doses can induce covert alterations in the organism which can later manifest as behavioral disturbances without gross functional impairment or structural birth defects. The overt damage to organs and to the nervous system is usually obvious, and its patterns are well known.

It is not generally recognized that the disturbances caused by such alterations are not necessarily obvious at birth, but emerge as the child grows older. Nor is it commonly appreciated that teratogens which have an affinity for developing brain centers may induce subtle alterations which may manifest in later life as behavioral disturbances and learning disabilities. In 1968 Nair and Dubois reported that a morphological or biochemical lesion may remain dormant and not be manifest as a behavioral disorder or functional impairment until later life. This may explain the delayed onset of the behavioral disturbance and learning disabilities so frequently noted when the history suggests possible intrauterine damage.

Relative to the mode of action of artificial food colors and flavors, there are two possibilities to consider. The food additives may play a primary role as the sole etiologic agent. Or, they may serve as irritants superimposed upon a substratum created by any one of the commonly cited causes of neurologic damage (Table I). In either situation, the toxicants may be ingested by the mother during pregnancy or encountered by the patient during extrauterine life.

Although it is possible that the artificial colors and flavors ingested by the mother may play a primary role in the induction of teratogenic alterations, there is as yet no supporting evidence for this concept. The primary extrauterine role is suggested by the complete reversal of all deficits, both behavioral and learning, following the elimination of the colors and flavors from the diet. The completeness of the favorable response and the ability to induce a rapid recurrence within hours indicate that this is a functional disturbance.

In addition to the functional disturbances induced by the artificial colors and flavors, it is conceivable that irreversible neurologic damage may result, particularly from continued exposure to the chemical over many years. Such damage could explain the persistence of various degrees of muscle incoordination and learning disabilities when a dramatic improvement in the behavioral pattern follows dietary management. Since the higher association centers are the last to differentiate, they are the most susceptible to neurotoxicants. In the human, these centers are not fully developed at birth and are ready targets for damage which can be manifest as the hyperkinetic syndrome. It is conceivable that the high incidence of failure to respond among adolescents may be attributed to irreversible neurologic damage.

As secondary agents acting upon pre-existing neuropathology, the synthetic colors and flavors can produce a variety of clinical patterns — e.g., the hyperkinetic syndrome, seizures labeled as petit mal, mental retardation, and learning disabilities. The secondary role is suggested by a history positive for neurologic damage attributed to other causes, and improvement of various degrees in response to dietary management.

For example, the elimination of colors and flavors may be followed by improved behavior but persistence of muscle incoordination with

perceptual and cognitive deficits. Seizures may be controlled without the use of drugs; but muscle incoordination and learning ability improve only partially or fail completely to respond. In retardation the clinical response may be dramatic, as evidenced by improved behavior, better coordination of both fine and gross muscles, and improved learning ability. All of these gains induce a marked transformation in the patient, whose expression becomes more alert and bright, his social adjustment improves, permitting him to function as a self-sufficient person who does not require one-to-one attention or instruction. In most patients labeled as "retarded," however, the level of learning ability usually remains below the normal estimated for age.

At times, residuals may persist with nothing in the history to suggest a cause. Behavioral toxicology is not yet sufficiently developed to provide guidelines for correlation of behavioral

patterns and learning disabilities with all of the potential neurotoxicants in the ecosystem.

CONCLUSION

Artificial food colors and flavors have the capacity to induce adverse reactions affecting every system of the body. Of all these adverse reactions, the nervous system involvement, as evidenced by behavioral disturbances and learning disabilities, is the most frequently encountered and most critical, affecting millions of individuals in this country alone.

The K-P Diet, which eliminates all artificial food colors and flavors as well as foods with a natural salicylate radical, will control the behavioral disturbance in 30 to 50% (depending upon the sample) of both normal and neurologically damaged children. — *Allergy Department, Kaiser-Permanente Medical Center, 2200 O'Farrell Street, San Francisco, Calif. 94115.*

Helping the Hyperkinetic Child

By ARNOLD H. ZUKOW, M.D.

Pediatrician, Encino, California, and Associate Clinical Professor of Pediatrics, UCLA School of Medicine.

Dr. Zukow spoke at greater length on this topic before the Nevada Academy of Family Physicians earlier this year.

Readers are invited to send in their reactions and comments on the article and/or on the subject of treating hyperkinetic children with drugs, a topic that has aroused considerable controversy in the press, despite the favorable experience of many physicians in using drugs such as Ritalin to treat so-called hyperkinetic disorders.

Dr. Zukow's views are in general agreement with the HEW Report of the Conference on the Use of Stimulant Drugs in the Treatment of Behaviorally Disturbed Young School Children, prepared by panelists from the fields of education, psychology, special education, pediatrics, adult and child psychiatry, psychoanalysis, basic and clinical pharmacology, internal medicine, drug abuse, and social work.

For further reading on the topic, see the bibliography at the end of the article.

Hyperkinetic children can have a negative effect on all those who care about them—especially their teachers. They have a short attention span and their actions are without direction, focus, or object. Their restlessness and impulsiveness disrupt discipline in the home and in the classroom. These children are often regarded as spoiled, ill-mannered, strange, or uncoordinated. They are in constant motion; have few friends; and exhibit temper tantrums, persistent sleep problems, learning problems, and aggressiveness.

These children frequently share two problems, both of which are developmental: social and occasionally physical immaturity and the inability to select discriminately from the stimuli in their environment.

They are not brain-damaged or psychotic. They do not possess an overt neurological syndrome, deafness, visual disability, or mental retardation. Their hyperactivity (always present in one degree or another in the hyperkinetic syndrome) should be viewed from a developmental frame of reference, i.e., the toddler is more restless and distractible than the school-age child, and the younger child is more distractible than the adolescent.

Unfortunately, the medical literature and lay press use the terms *hyperactive* and *hyperkinetic* interchangeably. In my opinion, they are not the same.

The problem which arises in using the terms *hyperactive* and *hyperkinetic* interchangeably is more than semantic. For instance, frustrated adults reacting to a child who does not meet their standards can easily exaggerate the significance of the child's occasional inattention or restlessness and label the youngster hyperkinetic.

A January 1971 HEW report on hyperkinesis says "the normal ebullience of childhood, however, should not be confused with the very special problems of the child with hyperkinetic behavior disorders." The report gives the following definition: "There is no known single cause or simple answer for such problems. The major symptoms are an increase of purposeless physical activity and a significantly impaired span of focused attention. The inability to control physical motion and attention may generate other consequences, such as disturbed moods and behavior within the home, at play with peers, and in the schoolroom."

This report further emphasizes the importance of the quality of hyperactivity. Children in whom the diagnosis is obvious are described as acting as if they possess an "inner tornado." The media have gone further, it seems to me, and have created a misleading stereotype of these children. They are depicted as the ones who destroy the supermarket, who set fire to sister's hair, the ones with clenched fists and bared teeth who seem to appear more animal than human.

It is true that some hyperkinetic children have signs of structural damage to their nervous system but most do not, and this point is very important.

I would describe hyperkinesis as a treatable illness characterized by involuntary behavior and/or learning problems in a child whose brain maturation is delayed. The history of the problem and the obvious tendency for a number of children identified as hyperkinetic to improve as they grow older supports this definition. An unknown number of children who have hyperkinesis and go untreated may certainly outgrow the syndrome without apparent sequelae.

The hyperkinetic child's inabil-

Helping the Hyperkinetic Child, Arnold H. Zukow, M.D., *Today's Education*, Vol. 64 No. 4, November/December, 1975. ©1975 NEA Journal.

Teachers can be important partners in identifying hyperkinetic children and in carrying out the proper therapy with them.

ity to control his or her span of concentration for a period of time long enough to assimilate and utilize incoming data results in uncontrolled emotional outbursts and emotional highs and lows. This leads to poor relationships with parents, teachers, and peers.

Identifying hyperkinetic children presents a perplexing problem. There is no way to identify and separate the children who would "naturally" outgrow the disability even if untreated from the ones who would develop serious emotional and learning deficits as a result of being untreated.

However, I would like to make several statements, based on my knowledge of and experience with hyperkinesis.

1. All hyperkinetic children are hyperactive.

2. All hyperactive children are not hyperkinetic.

3. All learning or behavior problems are not the result of hyperkinesis.

4. About 75 percent of hyperkinetic children do have a learning problem as a direct or indirect result of the condition. This is probably related directly to the intensity of either of the two (i.e., the child with a behavior problem can have a learning problem, which can lead to a greater behavior problem, which can similarly lead to a greater learning problem, etc.).

5. Learning disorders probably constitute the single most serious disability of childhood and have the greatest socioeconomic impact in adult life.

6. A youngster does not suddenly, at age six, become hyperkinetic. The signs are present very early in the child's life.

Medication prescribed by a qualified physician is valuable in the overall care of children with hyperkinesis because it reduces their excitability and impulsivity and increases their attention span and concentration. Specific stimulants can help these children improve their self-control and their relationships with those around them.

Many articles that have appeared in the nonprofessional press and even in many professional publications appear to have missed the object of drug treatment. The primary object of medication is not to calm these children. Rather it is to improve the functioning of their brain so that they can select from their environment the stimuli that will allow them to act appropriately in a situation. There are several well-documented studies which point out that the symptoms of hyperkinesis can be markedly improved by the judicious use of medications, especially methylphenidate.

Several researchers have clearly shown that not only are children on such medication less hyperactive, less belligerent, and more able to follow directions, but their attention span is improved and their distractibility is decreased. In addition, their coordination also improves if that was poor. There is, indeed, often a striking and at times almost unbelievable improvement in both the academic performance and the behavior of the children, which results in higher self-esteem and increased acceptance by their teachers and peers.

A case history will illustrate my point. When E. G., a six-and-a-half-year-old boy, became my patient, he was about to be expelled from school for kicking his classmates and the teacher. He was a bright child but was doing poorly in his schoolwork. He was hard to reason with at home, and he wanted to be the center of attention at all times. His peers avoided him whenever possible.

He was the product of a full-term uncomplicated pregnancy and was adopted by his parents at the age of three-and-a-half months. He had no history of serious trauma or serious illness, and his developmental milestones were normal.

I had his parents and teacher fill out evaluation forms about his behavior. On the school evaluation one, the teacher checked the column headed with one of the following, *never, almost never, sometimes, almost always,* or *always,* for statements such as "Finds it hard to play with peers" and "Reacts adversely to changes in routine." (The teacher's evaluation form has proved successful in informing teachers as well as in assessing the child's behavior.) On their form, the parents circled *yes* or *no* for statements such as "Short attention span," "Overly sensitive," "Panics easily," and "Quick-tempered."

After examination of the patient and the forms and after consultation with the parents, I prescribed Ritalin for E. G. The parents reported that after one week on the drug, his behavior had improved. A second teacher evaluation indicated great improvement in E. G.'s behavior.

After several months on Ritalin, he is a changed child—and all for the better, according to parents and teacher. His ability to make and maintain friends appears to be greatly improved and his ability to concentrate on schoolwork has also.

Generally speaking, when I prescribe Ritalin for a child, I begin with a very low dosage for five days of the first week. This enables parents and teachers to see differences in the child's behavior on and off the medication. Then I increase the dosage over the next two weeks.

I have contact with the parents at the end of each of these three weeks and then again at the end of six and 12 weeks. I advise parents that there may be several dosage changes until the most effective one is found.

The suggestion that the administration of this medication can lay the groundwork for future physical drug addiction is unfounded, in my opinion. As a matter of fact, many of these children resent the idea of having to take medication in order to function within their environment in an appropriate manner.

I believe that untreated youngsters who have had years of frustrating humiliation in the classroom and at home are much more likely candidates for addiction than are hyperactive children whose use of a drug has helped their self-control and ability to function in their environment.

Parents and teachers can, and must, be helped to view hyperkinesis as a treatable condition and to recognize that delayed brain maturation is not only an important but a common contributing factor to this syndrome. Then they will be more able to be understanding and patient with the hyperkinetic child.

Teachers and parents should give these children clear instructions and should avoid rigid scheduling of activities of fixed length. Their activities should be brief and should not exceed their capability for sustained attention.

When teachers detect early signs of an impending temper tantrum, they should take immediate steps to remove the child from the situation and offer an alternative distraction which could avoid the tantrum. However, once an explosion has occurred, there is nothing to do but wait it out, making sure that the child does not harm himself or herself or tyrannize others. This is about the same advice I would offer a parent or teacher dealing with a "normal" child who was having this type of behavior problem.

Teachers can be important partners in identifying hyperkinetic children and in carrying out the proper therapy with them—but only if they understand the problem and are willing to cooperate with doctor and parents. Teachers and doctor should focus on the ultimate goal: a child who is capable of functioning at his or her highest potential for learning within the classroom environment.

Teachers must be aware of their own abilities and limitations in dealing with the hyperkinetic child. Recognition of these abilities and limitations can only be helpful to teacher, child, and class.

If the hyperkinetic child gives any indication of having or developing a mental illness, the mental health profession should enter in the treatment. I often find a need for consultation from psychologists and psychiatrists in cases in which children are past the age of seven-and-a-half or eight, because they and their parents have had a greater chance of having suffered moderate to severe emotional sequelae as a result of the primary problem.

The mental health professional who becomes involved in such a case should have proper facilities for testing, evaluating, and treating. The treatment might involve medication, educational therapy, counseling by the child's doctor, family counseling by a mental health professional, or psychiatric counseling—any of these alone or in combinations, as appropriate.

One final point: If we, as teachers and physicians, can accept the fact that hyperkinetic children react to their environment in their own special way—*involuntarily*— we can understand and therefore we can help.

For Further Reading

Adler, S. *Your Overactive Child* New York: MEDCOM Press, 1972.

Conners, C. K., and Rothschild, G. H. "Drugs and Learning in Children" in *Learning Disorders*. J. Hellmuth (editor). Vol. III. Seattle: Special Child Publications, 1968.

Conners, C. K., and others. "Effects of Methylphenidate (Ritalin) on Paired-Associate Learning and Porteus Maze Performance in Emotionally Disturbed Children." *Journal of Consulting Psychology* 28:14-22; No. 1, 1964.

Laufer, M. W., and Denhoff, E. "Hyperkinetic Behavior Syndrome in Children." *Journal of Pediatrics* 50:463-74; April 1957.

Millichap, J. G. "Drugs in the Management of Hyperkinetic and Perceptually Handicapped Children." *Journal of the American Medical Association* 206: 1527-30; November 11, 1968.

Report of the Conference on the Use of Stimulant Drugs in the Treatment of Behaviorally Disturbed Young School Children, January 11-12, 1971. Washington, DC: Office of Child Development and Office of the Assistant Secretary for Health and Scientific Affairs, Department of Health, Education, and Welfare, 1971.

Safer, D. J. and Allen, R. P. "Factors Influencing the Suppressant Effects of Two Stimulant Drugs on the Growth of Hyperactive Children." *Pediatrics* 51: 660-67; April 1973.

Stewart, M. A., and others. "The Hyperactive Child Syndrome." *American Journal of Orthopsychiatry:* 36 861-67; No. 5, 1966.

Weiss, G., and others. "Comparison of the Effects of Chlorpromazine, Dextroamphetamine and Methylphenidate on the Behaviour and Intellectual Functioning of Hyperactive Children." *Canadian Medical Association Journal* 104: 20-25; January 9, 1971.

Influence of Fluorescent Lights on Hyperactivity and Learning Disabilities

John N. Ott, ScD

During the first five months of 1973, a pilot project was conducted by the Environmental Health and Light Research Institute in four first-grade windowless classrooms of a school in Sarasota, Florida. In two of the rooms, the standard cool-white fluorescent tubes and fixtures with solid plastic diffusers remained unchanged. In the other two rooms, the cool-white tubes were replaced with full-spectrum fluorescent tubes that more closely duplicate natural daylight. Lead foil shields were wrapped around each end of the tubes where the cathodes are located. Aluminum "egg crate" diffusers with an additional grounded aluminum screen grid replaced the solid plastic diffusers in these latter rooms. A dramatic improvement in behavior was demonstrated in hyperactive children.

Exploring the effect of lighting on behavioral problems is the newest emphasis for time-lapse photography at the Environmental Health and Light Research Institute. This is a report of a pilot project conducted in windowless elementary school classrooms by the Institute to study the effect of fluorescent lights on the behavior of children.

METHOD

Subjects for this study were children in four first-grade, windowless classrooms in Sarasota, Florida.

In two of the rooms the standard cool-white fluorescent tubes and fixtures with solid plastic diffusers remained unchanged.

In the other two rooms, the cool-white fluorescent tubes were replaced with full-spectrum fluorescent tubes that more closely duplicate natural daylight. Lead foil shields were wrapped around the cathode ends of the tubes to stop suspected soft X rays.

Procedure I. Special cameras were mounted near the ceiling in each of the four classrooms out of view of the children. The cameras were set to photograph sequences of time-lapse pictures during the school day.

Results. The photographs revealed the following: In the classrooms with standard unshielded fluorescent lights children could be observed fidgeting to an extreme degree, leaping from their seats, flailing their arms, and paying little attention to their teachers (see Figs. 1-3).

In the experimental classrooms the first graders settled down more quickly and paid more attention to their teachers. Less nervousness was evident and overall performance was better.

Procedure II. Full-spectrum shielded lighting was then installed in the two classrooms with standard lighting used in the earlier part of this study. Two and three months later the same children were photographed in the classroom in similar time-lapse pictures.

Results. The photographs revealed a very significant difference in the behavior of these children. They appeared calmer and more interested in their work. One little boy who stood out in the earlier films because he was constantly in motion and was inattentive had changed to a quieter child, able to sit still and concentrate on classroom routine. His teacher reported that he was capable of doing independent study now and that he had even learned to read during the short period of time (see Figs. 4, 5).

FIGURE 1. *Before lights were changed, note boy lower left banging head on table, boy upper center fumbling with chair and two on extreme right climbing on top of tables.*

DISCUSSION

The results of this study may indicate that hyperactivity is partly due to a radiation stress condition. Improvement in the children's behavior occurred when we eliminated excessive radiation and supplied that part of the visible spectrum which is lacking in standard artificial light sources.

Drugs and Hyperactivity. No drugs were administered in this study, and this is of

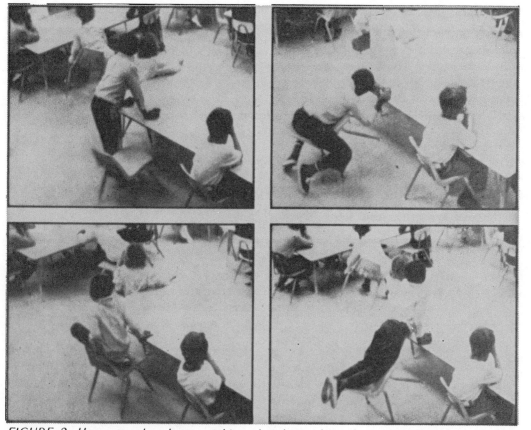

FIGURE 2. *How can a boy learn anything when he is obviously not paying attention to the teacher?*

particular significance since warnings are now being heard about the widespread use of amphetamines and other psychoactive drugs on children thought to be hyperactive. As child psychiatrist Mark Stewart of the University of Iowa pointed out in *Time Magazine* (Feb. 26, 1973), the danger is that "by the time a child on drugs reaches puberty, he does not know what his undrugged personality is."

Estimates of the number of children in this country now taking drugs range as high as 1,000,000, a situation which prompted the Committee on Drugs of the American Academy of Pediatrics to propose regulations to the U.S. Food and Drug Administration to prevent abuses (see *Time Magazine*, Feb. 26, 1973). Psychoactive drugs have been shown helpful in treating hyperkinesis, a restlessness that some

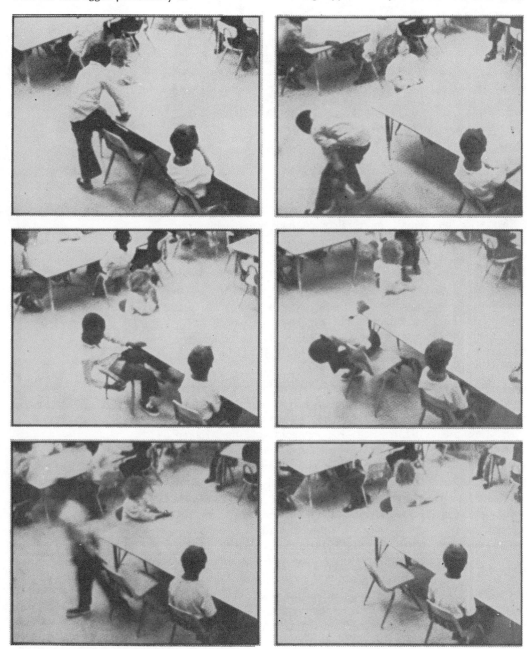

FIGURE 3. Will this boy ultimately become a dropout? See Figure 4.

FIGURE 4. No! 60 days after lights were changed this boy has moved up to the front row with his hand raised to gain recognition from teacher.

FIGURE 5. He is now at the blackboard, taking part in regular classroom activities.

experts believe derives from minimal brain damage or chemical imbalances. I worry for the future of the hyperactive boy we photographed and the many other children like him. If he gets relief through drugs from stress caused by malillumination and from radiation, will that lead to later addiction to drugs or alcohol? Irving Geller, chairman of the Department of Experimental Pharmacology at Southwest Foundation for Research and Education in San Antonio, has found that abnormal conditions of light and darkness can affect the pineal gland, one of the master glands of the endocrine system. Experimenting with rats, Geller (1971) discovered that rats under stress preferred water to alcohol until left in continuous darkness over weekends. Then they went on alcoholic binges. Nobel prize winner Julian Axelrod (1974) earlier found that the pineal gland produces more of the enzyme melatonin during dark periods. Injections of melatonin in rats on a regular light-dark cycle turned these rats into alcoholics.

Alcohol. I have found that many biological responses are to narrow bands of wavelengths within the total light spectrum. If these are missing in an artificial light source, the biological receptor responds as in total darkness. That alcoholism may be related to the pineal gland is also under study by Kenneth Blum, a pharmacologist at the University of Texas Medical School (see *Science News*, April 28, 1973).

Under near total darkness, rats with pineals drank more alcohol than water while rats without pineals drank more water than alcohol. When the animals were returned to equal periods of light and dark, rats with pineals retained their liking for alcohol. Applied to humans, Dr. Blum says "it is possible that alcoholics may have highly active pineals."

Artificial Food Flavors and Colorings. The hyperactive reaction to radiation from unshielded fluorescent tubes may have a correlation to the hyperactivity symptoms and severe learning disorders triggered by artificial food flavors and colorings (see *Newsweek*, July 9, 1973). Ben F. Feingold of the Kaiser-Permanente Medical Center in San Francisco found that a diet eliminating all foods containing artificial flavors and colors brought about a dramatic improvement in 15 of 25 hyperactive school children studied. Any infraction of the diet led within a matter of hours to a return of the hyperkinetic behavior (1973, 1975).

This points out the possibility of an interaction between wavelength absorption bands of these synthetic color pigments and the energy peaks caused by mercury vapor lines in fluorescent tubes. This could explain the reaction, or "allergy," to fluorescent lighting.

This could be eliminated two ways: by eliminating the absorbing material consumed when the child eats artificial coloring or by eliminating the culprit in fluorescent tubes. The fluorescent cathode as a source of soft X ray has been recognized by such scientists as K.G. Emeleus, professor of physics at Queen's University, Belfast, in his book, *The Conduction of Electricity through Gases.*

I first suspected soft X ray of having a deleterious effect on children as a result of time-lapse pictures that I made of flowers for the Barbra Streisand film "On a Clear Day You Can See Forever." Flowers nurtured under high-power fluorescent lights didn't grow as well near the ends of the tubes. Additional tests on bean sprouts showed abnormal growth in those near the ends of fluorescent tubes. With TV X ray measuring equipment, I have detected slight measurements of X rays at the ends of the tubes which would penetrate aluminum foil, but not lead foil.

The reaction to light energy through the eyes affecting the glandular system is being studied in another major research project being carried on by the Environmental Health and Light Research Institute. Anthony Marchese, working in the Department of Pharmacology at Stritch Medical School of Loyola University in Chicago, is studying the mechanism in the eye that responds to the pineal and pituitary glands which control basic body chemistry through production and release of hormones. Marchese has completed four years of medical school and is working on this project for his PhD dissertation.

The nonvisual response of the eye to wavelengths of light is why I have been so interested in the effects of tinted lenses, sunglasses, and artificial light sources that produce a distorted light spectrum entering the eye. By chance I observed that my arthritis improved when I lost my glasses and had to work in natural sunlight without them. I found that ordinary window glass and automobile windshields shut out up to 90% of the ultraviolet rays. I helped develop the full spectrum plastic lenses that are now available in clear and neutral gray. Contact lenses can also be ultraviolet-transmitting.

Radiation from TV Sets. My concern with the harmful effect of radiation from TV sets was tested in another school study, this time among hyperactive children placed at the Adjustive Education Center in Sarasota. TV sets in these children's homes which were found to be giving off measurable amounts of X radiation were either repaired or discarded. Sets were moved so that none would back up against a wall where anyone might be working or sleeping in the next room. Parents cooperated in

making their children sit back as far as possible and restricting the number of hours the children could watch TV.

The school principal reported that an improvement had been noted in the behavioral problems of the children in whose homes TV sets had been found which had been giving off radiation and which were repaired or removed. She noted that one of the most hyperactive children had been sleeping on the other side of a wall from a TV set giving off .3 milliroentgens of radiation per hour through the wall. This is within the "safety" standards of .5mrh set up by the 1968 Radiation Control Act. Without the TV radiation, this child improved so markedly she could return to her regular school.

Earlier research (Ott 1968 a, b) showed that young rats placed close to a color TV set with the picture tube covered with black photographic paper became highly stimulated, then progressively lethargic. All died in 10 to 12 days. Other recent experiments showed abnormal biological responses in plants left close to the ends of fluorescent tubes. The cathode there is basically the same as in a TV picture tube or X ray machine.

CONCLUSIONS

Under improved lighting conditions, using full-spectrum fluorescent tubes with lead foil shields over the cathode ends of the fluorescent tubes to stop soft X rays, children's behavior in the classroom showed dramatic improvement. On the basis of these findings, the Sarasota School Board has authorized an expanded comprehensive study. The proposed expanded study in nine windowless classrooms, kindergarten through second grade, will compare behavior patterns, scholastic achievement, attention spans, and general health under the improved lighting environment with present standard classroom lighting. — *Environmental Health and Light Research Institute, 1873 Hillview Street, Sarasota, Florida 33579.*

ACKNOWLEDGMENTS
The current school lighting study is made possible by grants to the Environmental Health and Light Research Institute from the Scott B. and Annie P. Appleby Foundation, Washington, D.C., and the Samuel J. and Evelyn L. Wood Foundation, Inc., New York City. The nonprofit Environmental Health and Light Research Institute is now seeking to raise additional funding on a wide-scale basis in order to expand the program.

My son, Henry, was in charge of the time-lapse camera work for this study and will be also for the expanded comprehensive study. Photos courtesy of the Environmental Health and Light Research Institute.

CONTROVERSIAL MEDICAL TREATMENTS OF LEARNING DISABILITIES

Robert L. Sieben

Robert L. Sieben, MD, 2425 East Street, Concord, California, 94520, is a consultant in pediatric neurology practicing in the San Francisco Bay Area. He is board certified in Pediatrics and Child Neurology and is a clinical instructor of neurology at the University of California Medical Center in San Francisco.

Parents are being inundated with medical advice about their learning-disabled children. This advice may come from well-meaning teachers, friends, or the media, and yet be rejected by the child's doctor. The resulting controversy is not in the child's best interest. This article is a physician's open critique of the popular medical treatments of learning disabilities recommended by some other physicians. It represents a point of view widely held by pediatricians but rarely expressed in the lay press.

Criteria for Evaluating Medical Advice

We must resist the temptation to follow each new treatment fad willy-nilly. We must realize that newspapers and news broadcasts are poor sources of medical information. Simplistic new theories offer hope and have news value, but their refutation is a tedious and thankless task which holds little interest for such media. The burden of proof is on the promotor of a new theory. It is up to him to perform the studies which test the validity of his hypothesis. It is up to him to convince his colleagues that he is on to something. To promote a hypothesis as fact without first submitting it to rigorous testing is a tremendous disservice to the patient and to the public. To recommend medical treatments of our children without first submitting these treatments to meaningful scientific scrutiny is an abuse of the very children we presume to be helping.

We should be alert for signs that a proposed treatment may be poorly substantiated. One such sign is the dramatic presentation of a new medical treatment directly to the public without opportunity for either peer review or rebuttal. Whereas this may impress the lay reader, such presentations may be based on distorted "medical facts" which are themselves quite debatable.

Another warning sign is the promoter's claim that there is a

"Controversial Medical Treatments of Learning Disabilities", Robert L. Sieben, *Academic Therapy,* Vol. 13, No. 2, November 1977, © 1977 Academic Therapy Publications, Inc.

medical conspiracy against a particular theory or treatment. What the medical promoter is really attacking is the "conspiracy" which requires him to test his own theory. His theory is not necessarily proven just because he has written a book about it. One can say virtually anything he wants to in his own book. He can do this in his most persuasive manner beyond the slightest scrutiny of his colleagues and without opportunity for rebuttal. A book is thus a very one-sided affair.

We should be particularly careful in drawing conclusions from anecdotal case reports. Clinical case histories suggest important new directions for investigation. They afford fresh insights into familiar problems. Yet they are by their very nature biased, subjective, and impressionistic. They contain no testable data and cannot be reproduced by other observers. Such cases are provocative, but they do not establish the validity of new treatments. We have been misled too many times to forego this key step.

CONTROVERSIAL THERAPIES

Dietary Treatments

Food additives. Food additives are considered by some to be the major cause of hyperactivity and learning disabilities. According to this theory all foods containing additives, dyes, or natural salicylates are to be excluded from the diet of the hyperactive learning-disabled child. These include all products containing any form of almonds, apples, apricots, berries, cherries, grapes, oranges, peaches, plums, tomatoes, cucumbers, luncheon meats, and colored cheeses, as well as most breads, cereals, bakery goods, desserts, candies, and beverages. Even mustard, catsup, oleomargerine, and colored butter are on the list. The mother is advised to make her own bakery items, ice cream, candies, mustard, and chocolate syrup. The child is not supposed to use any toothpaste, tooth powder, mouthwash, cough drops, throat lozenges, antacid tablets, or perfume. Practically all pediatric medications and vitamins, as well as most over-the-counter medications such as aspirin, are specifically forbidden.

The theoretical basis of this diet is developed by Benjamin Feingold, MD, in his book, *Why Your Child is Hyperactive* (1975). His hypothesis and the succession of anecdotal cases included in his book are certainly provocative. But, whereas he has recommended "the empirical application of dietary management to the hyperactive learning disabled, following what (he) considered to be sufficient substantiating evidence that the synthetic additives were involved," he does not share that substantiating data with us. He describes how his personal experience led him to discover his theory and develops a scientific basis for it. But he fails to provide us with objective data in support of his own hypothesis. There is no research design, description of population sample, or tabulation of results to review. The National Advisory Committee on Hyperkinesis and Food Additives (1975) reviewed his claims and found them impressionistic, anecdotal, and lacking in objective evidence.

There was a "demonstration study" performed April 15 to June 15, 1974, under the direction of the California State Department of Education which deserves considerable comment, for it supported the spread of Feingold's theories throughout the California public schools. Despite its widespread influence, the study is available only in mimeographed form. One of the stated purposes of this study was "to bring about a decrease in hyperactivity and generally improved behavior at school and at home for children diagnosed as hyperactive and put on the diet." The "field experimenter for the study, an experienced graduate teacher" found that sixteen of the twenty-five hyperactive children placed on the diet showed a "definite positive response with behavior change that was noticeable to parents, teachers, and the field experimenter." No further details regarding the specifics of the behavior change are given. Children's adherence to the diet was determined from questionnaires filled out by the parents and children without means of substantiation. The fact that the positive response coincided with the end of the school year was apparently considered to be of no significance. The considerable shortcomings of this study should be obvious to the thinking reader. Its stated purpose was to prove a point, and it was labeled "a demonstration study." A single teacher evaluated the results of this landmark study.

A controlled study has since been conducted by C. K. Conners, PhD (1976). Whereas he concluded that the Feingold diet may reduce hyperkinetic symptoms to a slight degree, even this improvement lasted only a few weeks. He felt further validation of the clinical effects was still required and expressed concern over his finding that the diet was somewhat less nutritious than the patients' regular diet.

There are substantial grounds for skepticism regarding Feingold's diet (Stare 1975). For one thing, it eliminates so many things that—even were it proven successful—one would still not really know which additives were the guilty ones. For another, it could be harmful in several ways. The teacher who recommends the diet does not have to implement it or endure the arguments that result from trying to persuade a child to follow it. Both parents and physicians may become quite upset with the teacher's attempt at "playing doctor." There is a real danger of such "treatment" becoming an easy way out of an educational problem for the school. Considerable time may be wasted in making repeated adjustments in the diet which could seriously delay more appropriate treatment. It may contribute to unwarranted parental feelings of guilt and inadequacy. One wonders how the child interprets the fact that he cannot eat the same as his peers, particularly when he is already considered different; otherwise, he would not be placed on the diet in the first place.

Brain allergies. The idea that the brain may be hypersensitive to certain foods and chemicals underlies the preceding treatment of learning disabilities. There are indeed patients with tension-fatigue syndrome who are irritable, tired, pale, and prone to headaches, stomachaches, and myalgia. They may or may not show the symptoms of hayfever. They respond to antihistamines and other treatments of allergies. That these symptoms may contribute to problems at school is not questioned.

But the idea that the brain itself is allergic is very misleading. For one thing, the lymphocytes which monitor the allergic response are prevented from entering the brain tissue by the blood brain barrier. For another, it is difficult to see how the typical case of hyperactivity or dyslexia could be caused by an allergy. Why are many hyperactive children already "spinning their wheels" before they have had their breakfast of presumed allergens? Why are boys more prone to learning disabilities when they are no more prone to allergic disorders? Children with the tension-fatigue syndrome are frequently seen by a child neurologist for evaluation of chronic headache. Yet these children are no more prone to dyslexia or hyperactivity than children with these latter disorders are prone to the tension-fatigue syndrome.

The treatments proposed for "brain allergy" are of no small concern. Frequent allergy shots may be prescribed at considerable cost and inconvenience to both the parent and child. Various elimination diets may be tried, with infinite variations that can delay more appropriate treatment for months and even years. Some have even recommended subjecting children with learning disabilities to hospitalization and allowing them nothing but water for four days, followed by gradual introduction of foods to determine sensitivities. At the least the child may be subjected to sublingual provocative doses of various dilutions of food extracts to both demonstrate and treat his food allergy—a practice shunned by most bona fide allergists as worthless and even dangerous (Breneman et al. 1974). The responses to these extracts are so nonspecific and subjective that they have not been found to be reproducible. Theoretical considerations militate against their validity (Golbert 1975).

One extreme to which the concept of brain allergy may be carried is demonstrated in R. C. Wunderlich's book, *Allergy, Brains, and Children Coping* (1973). This book is based on the debatable premise that "allergy can interfere with the function of the brain and the brain that doesn't work properly can bring on an allergy." No substantiation whatever is offered in support of this key statement. It is simply stated as fact, and the whole concept of the Neuro-Allergic Syndrome is built upon it.

It is reasoned that, since cortisone-like drugs (corticosteroids) are strong anti-allergy medicines, they can be very effective in treatment of the Neuro-Allergic Syndrome. The steroids are usually used for a few months to a year or so. There follows a series of 45 anecdotal case reports which comprise nearly two-thirds of the book's length. They describe dramatic improvement resulting from giving these medications to Neuro-Allergic Syndrome children with all of the following problems:

learning disorders	hyperactivity	skin rash
chronic irritability	delayed speech	eye strain
aggressive behavior	ear problems	stealing
recurrent fevers	constipation	dreaming

Steroids are potent drugs which reduce the allergic response. They are also hazardous drugs with many well known side effects. They weaken the body's defenses against infection to the point where chicken pox can become a fatal disease. They may soften bones so that spontaneous fractures of the back occur. They may stunt growth, produce ulcers, or even lead to damaging edema of the brain, to mention only a few of the possible side effects. Anecdotal case reports can scarcely be considered justification for their use.

Hypoglycemia. Another very popular explanation of learning disabilities is based on the concept of reactive hypoglycemia. A breakfast high in refined sugars first leads to an abrupt rise in blood sugar. This stimulates the pancreas to secrete insulin, which brings the blood sugar level down again by causing the body's cells to absorb the sugar, removing it from the blood stream. It is claimed by some that children with learning disabilities secrete too much insulin and overshoot the mark, leading to abnormally low levels of blood sugar. This is said to interfere with proper functioning of the brain by depriving it of sugar, its only source of energy. Yet no one has tested this hypothesis by measuring blood sugar or insulin levels in the classroom and correlating them with performance.

Breakfasts consisting largely of sugar have no staying power and may leave the child hungry and irritable within a few hours. This does seem to contribute to some children's difficulties in school. But the case for hypoglycemia has been very much overstated. If it is such a common cause of hyperactivity, why are boys so much more likely to be affected? Why is hyperactivity present after meals? Why are drugs which have a negligible effect on blood sugar sometimes helpful?

True reactive hypoglycemia is a rather rare condition. The low blood sugar is manifest two to four hours after a meal as fatigue, irritability, pallor, sweating, and fainting (Chutorian and Nicholson 1975). Since the body sees to it that the brain has first claim to whatever sugar is available, a truly hypoglycemic person would not be able to sustain the muscular effort required to be hyperactive. Diets high in refined sugar are fattening and bad for the teeth; but there is no evidence to support the widely publicized theory that reactive hypoglycemia causes learning disabilities. Neither is there anything to be gained by dietary measures directed toward bringing one's glucose tolerance test curve to some mythical ideal standard.

Megavitamins. Vitamins are complex organic substances found in most foods and essential in small amounts for the normal functioning of the body. Their absence from the diet leads to severe-deficiency diseases such as scurvy, rickets, and nervous system degeneration. The effect of vitamins on these diseases has been so spectacular that the public has long been captivated by their importance as part of the daily diet. Acceptance of vitamins as the virtual elixir of life has fostered a vast cult which believes that taking large doses of vitamins will help one achieve a mythical state of super-health. This has contributed to the advent of megavitamin therapy, which refers to the use of vitamins in quantities up to one thousand times the usual daily requirement. At these elevated doses any effects must be considered drug-like rather than nutritional.

Megavitamin therapy is the mainstay of orthomolecular psychiatry, whose proponents believe that mental illness may be treated by providing each cell in the body with the optimum environment of chemicals. Just how they determine what makes up that optimum environment remains a mystery. Whereas most vitamins are known to facilitate a multitude of chemical reactions within the body, there is still no evidence that massive amounts of vitamins "drive" these reactions in desirable directions. Initially, megavitamin therapy referred to the treatment of schizophrenia with large doses of niacin. Twenty years later this practice remains highly controversial. The claims of orthomolecular psychiatrists in the treatment of adult schizophrenia have been carefully examined in a report to the American Psychiatric Association by the Task Force on Vitamin Therapy in

Psychiatry (1974) and found those claims lacking in both reliability and specificity. This has not deterred the advocates of orthomolecular medicine who now claim that massive doses of several vitamins may be used for a wide range of problems including mental retardation, psychoses, autism, hyperactivity, dyslexia, and other learning disorders. This, in turn, has prompted the Committee on Nutrition of the American Academy of Pediatrics to publish a statement (1976) concluding that megavitamin therapy is not justified as a treatment for learning disabilities and psychoses in children.

There is nothing natural about extremely high doses of vitamins, yet many critics of food additives seem oblivious to the fact that these too are added chemicals, and they see nothing inconsistant in recommending them. This therapy appears to be based on the assumption that, if a small dose of something is good, a larger dose must be better. Salt is also essential to the body's proper functioning. Yet if one were to take such massive doses of salt it would be fatal!

The safety of massive doses of vitamins is by no means established. Little attention has been given to the potential toxicity of vitamins because no one anticipated that public figures would promote something as extreme as megavitamin therapy. Large doses of vitamin A are known to cause edema of the brain (Joint Committee 1971). The possibility of kidney stones must be considered in users of excessive amounts of vitamin C (Roth and Breitenfield 1977). Nicotinic acid and vitamin B_6 may cause liver damage. Is this only the beginning?

Trace minerals. Tests for trace minerals in the hair are the basis for a variety of treatments of presumed mineral imbalances. Whereas arsenic poisoning may be diagnosed by hair analysis even after death, and whereas rare disorders of copper and amino acid metabolism may produce characteristic abnormalities of hair structure, there is *no* data establishing that the pattern of trace elements present in one's hair has any relationship to clinical disease. To a degree it does represent what one has been eating. Hair analysis is a test that does not hurt and provides a wealth of impressive but useless chemical data. Any number of patterns are being described and related to a variety of ills by the orthomolecular psychiatrists as the basis for their treatments. Yet it has as much scientific validity as palmistry and phrenology.

Certain trace elements such as copper, zinc, magnesium, manganese, and chromium serve functions similar to vitamins and are essential to our health. It is nearly impossible, however, to avoid getting what one needs of these minerals through what one eats or drinks. Deficiency states are practically unknown, for they are truly required in very minute quantities. *No one* has published data supporting the theory that deficiencies in one or more of these elements may result in learning disabilities; yet children are being subjected to replacement therapy.

On the other hand, high levels of lead, mercury, iron, and other metals are known to be extremely toxic with devastating effects on the nervous system. It has not been established that hair analysis is useful in diagnosing these disorders. Nor has it been shown that small amounts of these elements are harmful. Children are being diagnosed by hair analysis as suffering from lead poisoning and are being placed on dietary treatments with large amounts of vitamin C by mouth as a chelating agent. Were they truly to have lead poisoning, this would constitute woefully inadequate treatment, for there is voluminous literature clearly establishing that these children require prolonged hospitalization with repeated injections of powerful chelating agents under close medical observation.

Neurophysiologic Retraining

These approaches are based on the idea that one can improve the function of a part of the central nervous system by stimulating specific sensory inputs, thereby eliciting specific motor output patterns. They include patterning, sensory integrative therapy, and optometric therapy.

Patterning. This technique is based on the theory that failure to pass properly through a certain sequence of developmental stages reflects poor "neurological organization" and may indicate "brain damage" (Delacato 1963). This developmental failure is overcome by flooding the sensory system with a structured program of stimulation in order to draw a response from the corresponding motor system. The therapeutic program is based upon an attempt to recapitulate the evolutionary stages of motor development through exercise. This is supposed to induce the nervous system somehow to make the proper neural connections, reorganize itself, and thus correct the presumed damage.

This "patterning" imposed upon the nervous system is claimed to be useful for (1) achieving greater ability in patients with brain damage; (2) treating communicative disorders such as visual, speech, and reading disabilities; (3) enhancing intelligence; and (4) preventing communicative disorders, altering deviant behavior, and improving coordination in normal subjects.

There is little doubt that extreme sensory deprivation, such as that caused by rearing animals in darkness, has important effects on neurological growth and development; however, less severe degrees of deprivation have not been shown to have any neurophysiological consequences. Furthermore, there is no evidence that any specific kind of replacement stimulation results in the rectification of neurological deficits once they have occurred (Cohen, Birch, and Taft 1970).

The "Doman-Delacato" treatment of neurologically handicapped children has been effectively refuted in a joint statement by the American Academies of Pediatrics, Neurology, Orthopedics, Cerebral Palsy, Physical Medicine and Rehabilitation, and the National Association of Retarded Children (1968). This statement is worth reading, not only for its criticism of this specific method of treatment, but as a model for evaluation of newer, controversial treatments. A careful review of the theory has led to the conclusion that "the tenets are either unsupported or overwhelmingly contradicted when tested by theoretical, experimental, or logical evidence from the relevant scientific literature. As a scientific hypothesis the theory of neurological organization seems to be without merit" (Robbins and Glass 1968).

Sensory integrative therapy. This approach to learning disabilities is based on the pioneering work of Jean Ayres, a doctor of psychology, who begins her classic text: "This book presents a neuro-behavioral theory. Theory is not fact but a guide for action. In this case the action is integrative therapy to assist children with learning deficits" (1972).

A theory is a plausible explanation of the relationship between observed facts. As a working hypothesis it serves to organize our thinking about a subject and point the way toward further research to test its validity. But it can scarcely be considered a guide to action until it has been proven a fact.

Ayres theorizes that learning disabilities may be due to deficits in the subconscious integrative mechanisms of the brain stem. This is the part of the nervous system which joins the brain to the spinal cord. The stimuli from the ears and eyes enter the brain stem and interact with sensory stimuli coming up from the arms and legs by way of the spinal cord. Much of the coordination of eye movements and much of the body's balancing system take place at this level. It remains to be shown, however, that children with learning disabilities have anything demonstrably wrong with their brain stems. The brain stem is rich in clinical signs readily apparent to a neurologist. The lack of any postmortem studies or accepted signs of brain-stem malfunction must lead one to seriously question Ayres' theory. Ayres further proposes that carefully controlled stimulation through the vestibular (balancing) and somatosensory (positional awareness) systems somehow improves the brain stem's integration between these systems and the eyes and ears. Just how stimulating these systems in certain ways is supposed to make them form the right nerve connections is not made clear.

There is no convincing evidence that mastering such postural skills carries over into academic skills such as reading (Silver 1975). Were it true, perhaps our gymnasts and tennis professionals should be running our school systems, for they have obtained enviable sensory integrative achievement.

Optometric training. We have seen how Doman and Delacato claimed to improve learning by patterning the brain and how Ayres formulated an action plan based on reorganizing the brain stem. Many developmental optometrists claim to achieve a similar goal by retraining the eye. Whereas most optometrists clearly limit their role in educational achievement to visual enhancement, others use a variety of expensive eye training techniques in an attempt to correct dyslexia and associated learning disabilities. The American Academy of Pediatrics, The American Academy of Ophthalmology and Otolaryngology, and the American Association of Ophthalmology issued a joint statement highly critical of this latter approach (1972). They concluded:

1. "Learning disability and dyslexia. . . require a multi-disciplinary approach from medicine, education, and psychology in diagnosis and treatment. Eye care should never be instituted in isolation when a patient has a reading problem."
2. ". . . There is no peripheral eye defect which produces dyslexia and associated learning disabilities."
3. "No known scientific evidence supports claims for improving the academic abilities of learning-disabled or dyslexic children with treatment based solely on:
   a. visual training (muscle exercises, ocular pursuit, glasses),
   b. neurologic organizational training (laterality training, balance board, perceptual training)."

4. "Excluding correctable ocular defects, glasses have no value in the specific treatment of dyslexia or learning problems."
5. "The teaching of learning-disabled and dyslexic children is a problem of educational science."

A variety of other methods have been advocated as treatment of learning disabilities. One of the more unbelievable consists of soaking flannel in castor oil, applying it to the abdomen, and heating it with an electric heating pad for an hour five times a week. This is supposed to somehow lubricate the lymphatics of the digestive system, improve the child's nutrition, and correct hyperactivity. Absurd? Of course! Yet hundreds of children have been treated in this way in suburban San Francisco at taxpayer expense. We can expect new theories and treatments to emerge over the next several years. Even chiropractors have entered the field. It is impossible to write a critique that will cover every possible treatment that is being proposed. The reader is cautioned to proceed with reason and not follow each new fad that comes along. We must not in our desperation allow our children to be the guinea pigs.

REAPPRAISAL OF THE PHYSICIAN'S ROLE

Considering that learning disabilities are primarily educational, social, and genetic problems rather than medical ones, it is quite reasonable to ask why a doctor should be involved at all. His involvement may be considered at several levels.

In the first place, the doctor *must* be involved if medications are to be given for management of hyperactivity, for he is the only one who may write the prescription. Certain medications may be quite helpful in eliminating hyperactivity and distractability contributing to learning disabilities. But this is not to say that their indiscriminate use is to be condoned. They are not a substitute for special education or a cureall for emotional problems. Their overenthusiastic use has led to a backlash of reaction which requires that we put them in proper perspective. They are short-acting drugs which may eliminate symptoms but which do not "cure" any "illness." The fact that they are used for social rather than purely medical reasons has led some to crusade against their use unreasonably. It should be pointed out that they may be stopped abruptly at any time without risk of withdrawal symptoms. Thus they could hardly be considered addictive in the way they are used for treatment of hyperkinesis. There is a widespread misconception that the use of these medications in childhood will lead toward experimentation with addictive drugs during adolescence. On the contrary, children taking prescribed medications such as these drugs, anticonvulsants, or insulin for long periods of time appear to have more respect for drugs and are less prone to abuse them. Workers in drug abuse clinics find that their patients seldom have a history of being on drugs prescribed for hyperactivity.

Second, the doctor should evaluate the child for underlying illness that could be contributing to his difficulty in school. Symptoms of minimal brain dysfunction, hyperactivity, and school failure are quite nonspecific and may be mimicked by many diseases. The wise tacher should realize his or her limitations in making a diagnosis and insist on a thorough medical evaluation. For example, the child may be tired because he is anemic or has heart disease. He may be irritable because of pin-worms, chronic tension-fatigue syndrome, or even a brain tumor. He may be inattentive because he cannot hear well or because of frequent brief lapses of awareness characteristic of some forms of epilepsy. His poor coordination may reflect a variety of neuro-muscular diseases. His poor enunciation may be a sign of cerebral palsy limited to the muscles of speech. There is a very real danger that diseases such as these will be mistaken for "MBD" (minimal brain dysfunction).

Third, the doctor may go a step further and explore his patient's psychosocial background. Anxiety, disruptive home life, and childhood neuroses may be reflected in problems at school. Stimulant medications are no more effective for these disorders than psychotherapy is for hyperactivity. In children with bona fide learning disabilities, serious emotional difficulties often result from the frustrations and failures they experience at school. These emotional problems further interfere with the child's learning and may seem to be the primary problem. The parents must therefore realize the tremendous importance of the child's feelings about himself as a person, for if his self-image is lost, the battle is lost. Psychotherapy may help the child cope, but a few hours of help per week can do little if the child is experiencing frustrations and failure the rest of the week both at school and at home.

The doctor knowledgeable about learning disabilities may even make an "educational" diagnosis. His limitations in this area should be obvious. Nonetheless, he is often forced into this role by default when the school is unaware of the problem, ignores it, or lacks the resources to deal with it. He may be able to muster special educational help for the child either within the school or from outside sources. This is particularly important when the child's disability is "minor" when compared to his more severely affected classmates, but still quite significant to himself and his parents. In other instances the physician may have to serve as a kind of referee when the parents are unwilling to accept that their child is less than perfect even though the school has ade-quately diagnosed his learning disability. Here the knowledgeable doctor may be able to substantiate the school's diagnosis and help the parents obtain better insight into their child's difficul-ties.

Thus far we have considered the doctor's role in evaluating a patient already suspected of having a learning disability. But he may also be the one who first suspects the diagnosis. For exam-ple, a child may develop severe headaches, recurrent vomiting, or dramatic behavior problems as a psychosomatic defence against what to him are impossible academic demands. In extreme cases children even develop hysterical paralysis, blindness, deafness, and seeming convulsions to avoid failing at school.

Summary

The preceding roles are reasonable ones for a doctor to fulfill in dealing with learning disabilities. As one can see, they are somewhat limited. It is unfortunate that the understandable desire of both parents and teachers to find a quick and easy cure has encouraged widespread acceptance of very dubious medical treatments. There is no such ready cure. The treatment of these problems is largely a laborious educational and social one.

Effects of Methylphenidate on Motor Skill Acquisition of Hyperactive Children

Michael G. Wade, PhD

This reports a study of the motor performance of 12 normal children and 12 hyperactive children with and without methylphenidate. The task required subjects to maintain their equilibrium on a square platform that rotated (+10 from horizontal) about a central axis. Subjects performed 30 trials at each of two testing sessions. Hyperactive subjects were receiving medication (methylphenidate) to control their hyperactivity on one of the test sessions, and a placebo on the other. The medicated hyperactive subjects performed more like their normal peers than did those receiving a placebo. This was true for both average performance scores and for consistency of performance.

Hyperactivity (also known as hyperkinesis, attentional deficit disorder, minimal brain dysfunction) is a common abnormality of children who are easily distracted, fidgety and disruptive in situations demanding high social compliance, and learning disabilities are a frequent consequence of this syndrome. It is estimated to occur in 3-10% of school children. There is general agreement that hyperactive children exhibit attentional deficits, but little empirical effort has been made to specify the nature of the attentional problems that seem to be present (Douglas 1972).

Knights and Hinton (1969) reported beneficial effects of methylphenidate with placebo control on a battery of tests, some of which measured fine motor coordination. Although children with learning disabilities have shown associated motor problems (Cratty 1970, Godfrey & Kephart 1969), no empirical evidence is available on the hyperactive subject's motor skill in tasks that present problems of locomotion and balance. Purposeful motor activity is an important ingredient for the developing child, and data on performance capabilities of hyperactive children in the motor domain are therefore important.

The present study investigated the motor performance of young hyperactive subjects under two conditions: on methylphenidate and on a placebo. Further, it compared their performance with that of a matched group of normal subjects. The task involved thirty 30-second trials with a 30-second intertrial interval (ITI). It would thus be considered an experimental task of relatively long duration, and hyperactive subjects who characteristically lack persistence might well experience difficulties toward the end of an experimental session. Methylphenidate is widely used by physicians as therapy in hyperactivity. If this medication *is* beneficial, it is logical to hypothesize that subjects would be more able to sustain their performance while on the medication. The experimental task was intended to test this hypothesis.

"Effects of Methylphenidate on Motor Skill Acquisition of Hyperactive Children", Michael G. Wade, Ph.D. *Journal of Learning Disabilities*, Vol. 9, No. 7, August/September 1976, ©1976 Professional Press, Inc.

SUBJECTS

Subjects were 12 hyperactive children and 12 normal children, matched by age and weight. All 24 children were of normal intelligence. The hyperactive children were selected from referrals to a psychopharmacological project* currently under way at the University of Illinois Institute for Child Behavior and Development. Before a child was considered as a potential subject and brought to the Institute for workup, he or she had been performing below academic capacity and had received a score of at least 15 on the Conners Teachers Rating Scale for Hyperactivity (Sprague, Christensen, & Werry 1974). A score of 15 is more than two standard deviations above the norm for the Champaign-Urbana community. Workup at the Institute by the research pediatrician confirmed the diagnosis of hyperactivity. The subjects ranged in age from 92 to 141 months ($\overline{X}$ = 121.8), and weighed between 25.2 and 38.1 kilograms ($\overline{X}$ = 31.20). Medication (methylphenidate) dosages ranged from .09 mg per kilo to 1.17 mg per kilo. Methylphenidate is a short-acting drug and the three-week time lag between subjects receiving active medication and placebo was a more than adequate washout period for this rapidly excreted drug. Data for this study were collected during the long-term follow-up of the subjects, and the dosage levels had been adjusted for each child to a level considered optimum by the research pediatrician.

PROCEDURE

The apparatus and recording system have been described more fully elsewhere (Wade & Newell 1972). The task required the subject to balance in the lateral plane on a 3- by 3-foot board which rotated about a central steel shaft. The board deflected $\pm 10°$ from the horizontal position. The object of the task was to balance for as much of a 30-second trial as possible. At the end of the trial, the subject sat down and received knowledge of results (KR) halfway through the intertrial interval (ITI). KR was the time in balance (TIB) during the previous trial to the nearest tenth of a second. The subject performed 30 trials to complete an experimental session. The hyperactive subjects received their medication one and a half hours prior to participation in the experiment.

On entering the test area, the experimenter familiarized the subject with the task, pointing out the appropriate foot placement and em-

phasizing the task objective. When the experimenter was satisfied that the subject understood the task objective, the experimental session commenced.

ANALYSIS AND DESIGN

The experimental design was a single, fixed-effects model to include all effects which might systematically influence the subject's behavior as measured by random variables (Y) which are functions of the subject's time-in-balance score. The model represents an estimate (E) of Y as: $E(Y) = M \pm S \pm B \pm K + e$. Thus, for normal subjects:

Effect	degrees of freedom
M = grand mean	
S = session	1
B = trial/blocks	2
K = effect due to children	11
e = error (independent and random with mean of zero and variance unknown)	54

With the rank of the matrix equal to 14 and 69 total observations, the degrees of freedom for error = 54.

The model for the hyperactive subjects was the same as the normal subjects' model with the addition of a drug effect (D) and a drug by blocks (DXB) interaction. Thus, $E(Y) = M \pm S \pm D \pm B \pm K \pm (DXB) + e$. This reduced the degrees of freedom for error by 3, the drug effect accounting for one degree of freedom and the interaction two degrees of freedom. With the rank of the matrix 17 and the total number of observations = 60, the degrees of freedom for error = 51.

With the relatively small number of hyperactive subjects available for the study, the sensitivity of the experiment was safeguarded by considering the children as a fixed effect in the model and removing the effect of children in the analysis. No inferences regarding the variability due to the children were made except as a fixed effect.

Subjects were tested on two occasions and the methylphenidate or placebo was randomly assigned such that on the first testing session the subject was on one and on the second on the other. Two measures were recorded for analysis — the mean TIB scores, and the variance scores (i.e., subject's standard deviation about his own mean score within a block). The TIB scores indicated performance gain and the variance scores indicated the consistency of performance. For the analysis, the 30 trials were treated as three blocks each of ten trials.

*That research project (PHS Grant No. MH18909) is investigating the effects of methylphenidate on a wide variety of behavioral measures on children diagnosed as hyperactive.

2. HYPERACTIVE

TABLE I. Mean performance scores.

(a) TIME IN BALANCE

	Drugs		Placebo		Normal	
	Session$_1$	S$_2$	S$_1$	S$_2$	S$_1$	S$_2$
Block 1	11.57	14.22	10.76	13.00	12.90	16.50
Block 2	12.77	15.26	11.18	14.88	14.12	18.30
Block 3	14.44	14.75	11.77	13.97	16.06	19.05
	12.93	14.74	11.24	13.95	14.36	17.95

(b) VARIABILITY SCORES

Block 1	2.85	2.07	2.90	3.18	3.27	3.21
Block 2	3.34	2.75	2.84	6.31	2.14	2.10
Block 3	3.44	1.52	4.00	3.71	2.54	2.56
	3.21	2.12	3.25	4.40	2.65	2.62

RESULTS

Table I shows the average scores for both the time in balance (TIB) and the variability scores. For the TIB scores (Table Ia) all the hyperactive subjects, both those on medication and those on placebo, improved over the two sessions as did the matched normal group. Average performance was higher for the hyperactive subjects while on medication than on placebo, irrespective of session. The matched normal group performed at a significantly higher level than the hyperactive subjects. The variability scores (Table Ib) indicate performance consistency, and here the hyperactive subjects on medication were more consistent in their performance across the two sessions than on placebo. The performance variability of the matched normal group was essentially the same as that of the hyperactive subjects while on medication. Illustrated in Figure 1 are both the average TIB scores and the variance scores. The performance of the matched normal subjects was superior to that of the hyperactive subjects both on medication and on placebo.

It should be noted that the hyperactive subjects on placebo decreased their TIB performance during the last 10 trials of a session (block 2 to block 3). Performance consistency for the normal and hyperactive subjects on medication was essentially the same, with the hyperactive subjects on placebo much less consistent in their performance.

Direct statistical comparison between the matched normal group and the hyperactive subjects was not appropriate and separate variance analyses were computed. For the normal subjects the effects of session and trial/block were both significant ($p < .01$) as might be expected, with subjects performing better on the second testing session and block 3 in both of the 30 trial sessions. The variance scores (SD of subject about his own mean score) showed the normal subjects improving their performance consistency ($p < .05$) over blocks as they learned the skill. No significant difference between the two testing sessions was apparent.

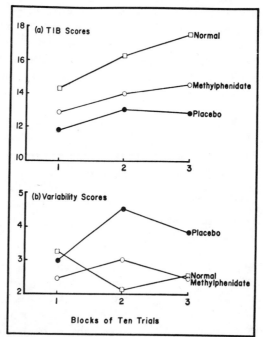

FIGURE 1. Mean performance scores (seconds) summed across sessions.

For the hyperactive subjects the session effect was significant ($p < .01$) and, as illustrated in Figure 1, the hyperactive subjects on methylphenidate performed at a higher level than when on placebo ($p < .01$). Variability scores for the hyperactive subjects indicated a significant effect for medication ($p < 10$). Although below a conventional (.05) alpha level, these data suggest greater variability in performance by subjects off medication. In the lower portion of Figure 1 the normal subjects and hyperactive subjects are essentially the same in performance consistency. No other F-ratios were significant for the hyperactive subjects ($p > .05$).

DISCUSSION

Hyperactive subjects on placebo were less consistent in their performance than when on methylphenidate, and this variability tended to increase during a 30-trial testing session. As Figure 1 illustrates, hyperactives on placebo did not increase their TIB scores (Fig. 1a) from block 2 to block 3, and during that period their performance consistency (Fig. 1b) was lower (higher variability) than earlier in the sessions. These data agree with data on a wide range of cognitive tasks reported by Douglas (1972) and Sprague and Sleator (1973). Implicit here is the notion that acquiring a motor skill involves cognitive activity similar to that of performing a memory task, or watch-keeping, in that information must be attended to and an appropriate response produced.

The highly significant effect of medication suggests that methylphenidate administered to the hyperactive subjects enabled them to produce motor skill behavior that not only approximated the matched normal group in absolute magnitude, but more importantly was characteristic of the normal group's performance. That is, performance consistency increased over trials for the hyperactive subjects receiving medication. In this study the hyperactive children on placebo performed less well than their normal peers although both groups were in the same intelligence range. The hyperactive children receiving medication showed performance characteristics similar to the normal group. The data agree with the results of Knights and Hinton (1969). They interpreted longer duration scores on tests of fine motor coordination as improved attention span and attributed this to the effects of methylphenidate. Better performance on the present task by hyperactive subjects is interpreted in the same manner. The administration of methylphenidate to correctly diagnosed hyperactive children is beneficial in performing motor skills which involve repeated responses and error correction to increase level of performance.

Investigations of the motor skill capabilities of hyperactive children is sparse, both in terms of their performance as a special group and the effects of methylphenidate. The results of the present study point to two conclusions. First, untreated young hyperactive children experience difficulties with motor skill learning in very much the same fashion as they do with other cognitive tasks. Second, the use of methylphenidate aids in motor skill learning for hyperactive children. — *Leisure Behavior Research Lab, 95 Institute for Child Behavior and Development, 51 Gerty Drive, Champaign, Ill. 61820.*

INDEX

STAFF

Publisher	John Quirk
Editor	Dona Chiappe
Editorial Ass't.	Carol Carr
Permissions Editor	Audrey Weber
Director of Production	Richard Pawlikowski
Director of Design	Donald Burns
Customer Service	Cindy Finocchio
Sales Service	Diane Hubbard
Administration	Linda Calano
Index	Mary Russell

Cover Design	Donald Burns
Cover Photo	Richard Pawlikowski

Appendix: Agencies and Services for Exceptional Children

Alexander Graham Bell Association for the Deaf,
Inc.
Volta Bureau for the Deaf
3417 Volta Place, NW
Washington, D.C. 20007

American Academy of Pediatrics
1801 Hinman Avenue
Evanston, Illinois 60204

American Association for Gifted Children
15 Gramercy Park
New York, N.Y. 10003

American Association on Mental Deficiency
5201 Connecticut Avenue, NW
Washington, D.C. 20015

American Association of Psychiatric Clinics for
Children
250 West 57th Street
New York, N.Y.

American Bar Association
Commission on the Mentally Disabled
1800 M Street, NW
Washington, D.C. 20036

American Foundation for the Blind
15 W. 16th Street
New York, N.Y. 10011

American Medical Association
535 N. Dearborn Street
Chicago, Illinois 60610

American Speech and Hearing Association
9030 Old Georgetown Road
Washington, D.C. 20014

Association for the Aid of Crippled Children
345 E. 46th Street
New York, N.Y. 10017

Association for Children with Learning Disabilities
2200 Brownsville Road
Pittsburgh, Pennsylvania 15210

Association for Education of the Visually
Handicapped
1604 Spruce Street
Philadelphia, Pennsylvania 19103

Association for the Help of Retarded Children
200 Park Avenue, South
New York, N.Y.

Association for the Visually Handicapped
1839 Frankfort Avenue
Louisville, Kentucky 40206

Center on Human Policy
Division of Special Education and Rehabilitation
Syracuse University
Syracuse, New York 13210

Child Fund
275 Windsor Street
Hartford, Connecticut 06120

Children's Defense Fund
1520 New Hampshire Avenue NW
Washington, D.C. 20036

Closer Look
National Information Center for the Handicapped
1201 Sixteenth Street NW
Washington, D.C. 20036

Clifford W. Beers Guidance Clinic
432 Temple Street
New Haven, Connecticut 06510

Child Study Center
Yale University
333 Cedar Street
New Haven, Connecticut 06520

Child Welfare League of America, Inc.
44 East 23rd Street
New York, N.Y. 10010

Children's Bureau
United States Department of Health, Education
and Welfare
Washington, D.C.

Council for Exceptional Children
1411 Jefferson Davis Highway
Arlington, Virginia 22202

Epilepsy Foundation of America
1828 "L" Street NW
Washington, D.C. 20036

Gifted Child Society, Inc.
59 Glen Gray Road
Oakland, New Jersey 07436

Institute for the Study of Mental Retardation
and Related Disabilities
130 South First
University of Michigan
Ann Arbor, Michigan 48108

International Association for the Scientific Study
of Mental Deficiency
Ellen Horn, AAMD
5201 Connecticut Avenue NW
Washington, D.C. 20015

International League of Societies for the Mentally
Handicapped
Rue Forestiere 12
Brussels, Belgium

Joseph P. Kennedy, Jr. Foundation
1701 K Street NW
Washington, D.C. 20006

League for Emotially Disturbed Children
171 Madison Avenue
New York, N.Y.

Muscular Dystrophy Associations of America
1790 Broadway
New York, N.Y. 10019

National Aid to the Visually Handicapped
3201 Balboa Street
San Francisco, California 94121

National Association of Coordinators of State
Programs for the Mentally Retarded
2001 Jefferson Davis Highway
Arlington, Virginai 22202

National Association of Hearing and Speech
Agencies
919 18th Street NW
Washington, D.C. 20006

National Association for Creative Children and
Adults
8080 Springvalley Drive
Cincinnati, Ohio 45236
(Mrs. Ann F. Isaacs, Executive Director)

National Association for Retarded Children
420 Lexington Avenue
New York, N.Y.

National Association for Retarded Citizens
2709 Avenue E East
Arlington, Texas 76010

National Children's Rehabilitation Center
P.O. Box 1260
Leesburg, Virginia

National Association for the Visually Handicapped
3201 Balboa Street
San Francisco, California 94121

National Association of the Deaf
814 Thayer Avenue
Silver Spring, Maryland 20910

National Cystic Fibrosis Foundation
3379 Peachtree Road NE
Atlanta, Georgia 30326

National Easter Seal Society for Crippled Children
and Adults
2023 W. Ogden Avenue
Chicago, Illinois 60612

National Federation of the Blind
218 Randolph Hotel
Des Moines, Iowa 50309

National Paraplegia Foundation
333 N. Michigan Avenue
Chicago, Illinois 60601

National Society for Autistic Children
621 Central Avenue
Albany, N.Y. 12206

National Society for Prevention of Blindness, Inc.
79 Madison Avenue
New York, N.Y. 10016

Orton Society, Inc.
8415 Bellona Lane
Baltimore, Maryland 21204

President's Committee on Mental Retardation
Regional Office Building #3
7th and D Streets SW
Room 2614
Washington, D.C. 20201

United Cerebral Palsy Associations
66 E 34th Street
New York, N.Y. 10016

SPECIAL EDUCATION SERIES

- ● Autism
- * ● Behavior Modification
- Biological Bases of Learning Disabilities
- Brain Impairments
- ● Career and Vocational Education
  for the Handicapped
- Child Abuse
- Child Development
- Child Psychology
- Cognitive and Communication Skills
- * ● Counseling Parents of Exceptional
  Children
- Creative Arts
- Curriculum and Materials
- * ● Deaf Education
- Developmental Disabilities
- * ● Diagnosis and Placement
- Down's Syndrome
- ● Dyslexia
- Early Learning
- Educational Technology
- * ● Emotional and Behavioral Disorders
- Exceptional Parents
- * ● Gifted and Talented Education
- * ● Human Growth and Development of
  the Exceptional Individual
- Hyperactivity

- * ● Individualized Educational Programs
- ● Language & Writing Disorders
- * ● Learning Disabilities
- Learning Theory
- * ● Mainstreaming
- * ● Mental Retardation
- ● Motor Disorders
- Multiple Handicapped Education
- Occupational Therapy
- ● Perception and Memory Disorders
- * ● Physically Handicapped Education
- * ● Pre-School Education for the Handicapped
- * ● Psychology of Exceptional Children
- ● Reading Disorders
- Reading Skill Development
- Research and Development
- * ● Severely and Profoundly Handicapped
- Slow Learner Education
- Social Learning
- * ● Special Education
- * ● Speech and Hearing
- Testing and Diagnosis
- ● Three Models of Learning Disabilities
- * ● Visually Handicapped Education
- * ● Vocational Training for the Mentally
  Retarded

● Published Titles   * Major Course Areas

Exceptional Children:
A Reference Book

**An updated and welcome resource
for educators and librarians.**

COMMENTS PLEASE:

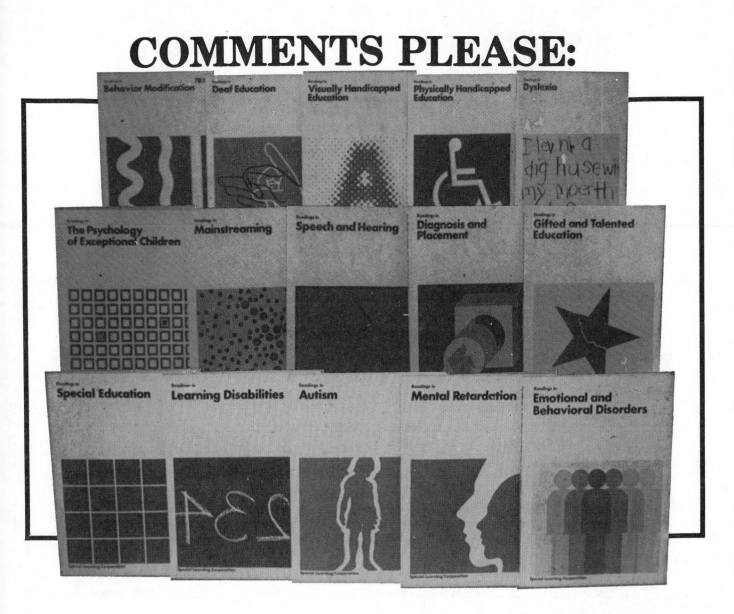

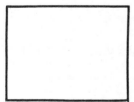

SPECIAL LEARNING CORPORATION
42 Boston Post Rd.
Guilford, Conn. 06437

SPECIAL LEARNING CORPORATION
COMMENTS PLEASE:

Does this book fit your course of study?

Why? (Why not?)

Is this book useable for other courses of study? Please list.

What other areas would you like us to publish in using this format?

What type of exceptional child are you interested in learning more about?

Would you use this as a basic text?

How many students are enrolled in these course areas?

_____ Special Education _____ Mental Retardation _____ Psychology _____ Emotional Disorders

_____ Exceptional Children _____ Learning Disabilities _____ Other _____

Do you want to be sent a copy of our elementary student materials catalog?

Do you want a copy of our college catalog?

Would you like a copy of our next edition? ☐ yes ☐ no

Are you a ☐ student or an ☐ instructor?

Your name _____ school _____

Term used _____ Date _____

address _____

city _____ state _____ zip _____

telephone number _____

M/D